RED, WHITE, AND 'QUE

RED, WHITE, AND 'QUE

Farm-Fresh Foods for the American Grill

BY KAREN ADLER AND JUDITH FERTIG

RUNNING PRESS
PHILADELPHIA

Books published by Running Press are available at special discounts for bulk purchases in the
United States by corporations, institutions, and other organizations. For more information, please
contact the Special Markets Department at Perseus Books, 2300 Chestnut Street, Suite 200,
Philadelphia, PA 19103, or call (800) 810-4145, ext. 5000, or e-mail special.markets@perseusbooks.com.

ISBN 978-0-7624-6129-5
Library of Congress Control Number: 2016960197

E-book ISBN 978-0-7624-6130-1

9   8   7   6   5   4   3   2   1
Digit on the right indicates the number of this printing

Designed by Amanda Richmond
Edited by Kristen Green Wiewora
Food Styling by Mariana Velasquez
Prop Styling by Kristi Hunter
Typography: Burford, Eames Century Modern, and Neutra Text

Running Press Book Publishers
2300 Chestnut Street
Philadelphia, PA 19103-4371

Visit us on the web!
www.offthemenublog.com

★ ★ ★

To farmers and gardeners,
barbecuers and grillers,
makers and enjoyers.

TABLE *of* CONTENTS

ACKNOWLEDGMENTS

We wish to thank the Kansas City Barbeque Society (KCBS) and our fellow Ph.B. faculty members at the fictitious but delicious Greasehouse University. Likewise, we appreciate all the gardening experts, farmers, ranchers, fishing industry professionals, and artisan producers who have helped create a vast and diverse array of foods to sizzle and smoke.

We wouldn't have this book without our savvy agents Lisa Ekus and Sally Ekus, our wonderful editor Kristen Green Wiewora, designer Amanda Richmond, photographer Steve Legato, publicist Seta Zink, and everyone at Running Press.

And we toast each other. As barbecue co-authors, we each bring a little something different to the table. And we're still friends!

THREE CHEERS FOR THE
RED, WHITE, AND 'QUE!

Red, White, and 'Que celebrates a can-do, roll-up-your-sleeves spirit, taking your grilling, slow smoking, planking, and grill-roasting to the next level. Wherever you build your fire—in a driftwood pile on the beach, a fire pit by a lakeside cabin or a tent in the woods, a grill in a backyard, or a smokin' cooker at a barbecue competition—you now have over 100 recipes to rev up your repertoire.

This book is where innovation—you can grill *that*?—meets time-honored tradition to deliver big-time flavor.

Red, White, and 'Que is about making the most of farm-fresh, seasonal ingredients, from the first asparagus of spring in Purple, Green, and White Asparagus with Grilled Lemon Butter (page 142) to summer's Stars and Stripes Grilled Banana Split (page 187) to a whole, fabulous stalk of Ember-Roasted Brussels Sprouts (page 146) in fall and Grilled Butternut Squash with Garlic and Olives (page 156) in winter.

You can take foods you've grown yourself or "harvested" from your local farmers' market and make them better yet. A little heat and a little smoke are all it takes. Smoked Applesauce (page 130) or Grilled Kale Bundles topped with Warm Cranberry-Bourbon Vinaigrette (page 94)? Yeah, baby! Blistered Green Beans with Buttermilk Ranch Dressing (page 88) takes that ubiquitous vegetable we all think we know, adds a retro salad dressing that yearns to be rediscovered in its homemade form, and combines for a dish that everyone will love. Ruby Slipper Beets (page 144) with a lick of

raspberry will take you somewhere over the rainbow. Chars and Stripes Grilled Vegetable Platter (page 162) allows you to celebrate the blue-ribbon winners from your local farmer.

You can also discover new ways to slow smoke a brisket (page 122) or plank salmon (page 110) or sizzle those ribs to a tender, juicy turn (page 125). You can rediscover classics like Green Goddess Dressing (page 82), which is delicious on just about anything you can grill. Bottle your own signature Cherry Chipotle Barbecue Sauce (page 128), so good you'll steal a spoonful of it from the refrigerator even when you're not grilling or smoking.

Nothing says "regional" like local wood: maple in New England, hickory in the South and Midwest, oak and mesquite in Texas, apple and cherry in the Great Lakes, live or red oak in California, cedar and fruitwoods in the Pacific Northwest. Wood is a great way not only to emphasize regionality but also give foods that aromatic taste of place. In *Red, White, and 'Que*, we give you lots of ways to use wood, no matter what kind of equipment you have. You can use wood for planking, wood grilling, grilling with a kiss of smoke, or slow smoking.

ABOUT THAT 'Q

No matter how you say it—or spell it—
Barbecue
Barbeque
Bar-B-Q
BBQ
Or simply Q—
Barbecue is a distinctly American contribution to the world's culinary traditions. Slow-smoked barbecue is all about turning bland and tough cuts of meat into tender, delicious, aromatic masterpieces with the ancient flavor of the hearth. Edward Lee writes in his cookbook *Smoke and Pickles*, "Some say umami is the fifth flavor, in addition to salty, sweet, sour, and bitter." The Korean-American chef with the yen for Southern barbecue goes on to suggest a sixth: smoke. Smoke flavor is a combination of bitter and the aroma from smoldering wood, a scent that can touch the most ancient part of the brain: the limbic system. Smoke deepens the flavor of any food it infuses.

In *Red, White, and 'Que*, we judiciously add smoke to cashews (Smoked Cashew Crema, page 72), apples (Smoked Applesauce, page 130), and beans (Barbecuer's White Bean Casserole, page 143), among others.

Back in the day, the only smoky condiments to choose from included a can of chipotle peppers, a little bottle of liquid smoke, and a hickory-smoked salt. Today, we're spoiled for choice. And that's because we've fallen in love again with smoke as a flavor. You can add a nuance of flavor with artisan products such as Cherry Smoked Honey from Bee Local in Oregon. Wood + Salt in Missouri offers many smoked products, including Tellicherry Rye Peppercorns, soaked in rye whiskey and then smoked over pecan wood, and Winter Smoked Sea Salt, which is smoked over smoldering cinnamon sticks, brown sugar, tea leaves, and orange zest. Bourbon Barrel Foods in Kentucky offers an array of bourbon-smoked products, including sea salt, pepper, paprika, chili powder, sesame seeds, and even cacao nibs. Smoked Spanish paprika was a hard-to-come-by condiment a few years ago and now is available from even McCormick at many grocery stores. Experiment as we do and add one of these smoky condiments in place of a non-smoked item to get that extra smokiness. So, let's learn something new. Keep getting better. Push the envelope. And let's raise the flag for the *Red, White, and 'Que!*

RED, WHITE, AND 'QUE TECHNIQUES

GRILLING IS A MATTER OF DEGREES

You can do a lot more with your grill than simply sear: You can melt, toast, scorch, blacken, blister, add a kiss of smoke, roast, plank, and grill in a flash. But first you need a grill.

GAS OR CHARCOAL GRILL?

People always ask us if we grill with charcoal or gas, to which we answer yes—we use both. The majority of American households have at least one outdoor grill, which, more often than not, is gas rather than charcoal. As far as we're concerned, to get great flavor and char, charcoal is the way to go—in particular, hardwood lump charcoal, which burns really hot for a terrific sear. But there are pluses to gas grilling as well, not the least of which is you just flip a switch and it's on. You can add wood smoke to a gas grill, too, as we'll show you later on. Just make sure you buy a unit with as high a number of BTUs (British Thermal Units, which measure the maximum heat output of a burner) as your budget permits for hot-surface searing. You'll need at least 40,000 BTUs from the grill burners (not including any side burners) to get good grill marks on your foods.

⟶ UTENSILS FOR RED, WHITE, AND 'QUE ⟵

Several basic tools make grilling easier. Kitchen shops, hardware stores, restaurant supply stores, or barbecue and grill retailers are good sources of the items listed below. Professional utensils are superior in quality and durability and worth the extra money. Long handles are preferable on everything, to keep you a safe distance from the fire.

Perforated grill racks are placed on top of the grill grates to accommodate small or delicate food items (such as chicken wings, fish fillets, shellfish, and vegetables) that might fall through the grates. Always oil the grill rack before using so that the food won't stick.

Cast-iron skillets, ovenproof skillets, and grill griddles are great for grilling flatbreads, steaks, chops, and fish fillets on the grill.

Grill woks and baskets with perforated holes let in smoky flavor while sitting directly on top of the grill. Stir-grill fish or shellfish, chicken, and vegetables by tossing them with long-handled wooden paddles.

Heat-resistant oven or grill mitts offer the best hand protection, especially when you need to touch any hot metal, such as skewers, during the grilling process.

Long-handled, spring-loaded tongs are easier to use than the scissors type. They are great for turning shellfish, sliced vegetables, and skewers. Buy two sets of tongs—one for raw meats and the other for cooked meats.

Long-handled offset spatulas with extra-long spatula surfaces are great for turning large pieces of food, such as fish fillets and long planks of eggplant, zucchini, or yellow squash. Oil the food well to avoid sticking.

Meatball grilling baskets are a necessity for handling meatballs. Ever try to grill meatballs on a grill rack? They escape like spooked cattle on the range during a storm. Like a skilled cowboy, you need to wrangle them into a meatball grilling basket, and then grilling and turning them is easy.

Skewers—wooden or metal—allow smaller items to be threaded loosely together and then placed on the grill to cook. Wooden or bamboo skewers should be soaked for at least 30 minutes before using so that the ends won't char during grilling. Flat wooden or metal skewers are preferred so that cubed food doesn't spin while turning. Or use double skewers to keep cubed food from spinning.

Disposable aluminum pans are perfect for grilling a medley of vegetables or catching the drippings under a spit-roasted chicken. Double them—i.e., put one on top of the other—when the food seems too heavy to safely maneuver in one pan.

An instant-read thermometer is good to have handy by the grill to test the doneness of beef, chicken, lamb, pork, turkey, and breads.

A charcoal chimney or electric fire starter is key for starting a charcoal fire.

A good-quality chef's knife is essential for preparing vegetables, fruits, herbs, and other foods destined for the grill.

Keep **a spray bottle or pan** filled with water handy to douse big flare-ups. (Little flare-ups add that bit of desirable char, and you want to be careful not to put out the fire.)

⟶ CLEANING AND MAINTENANCE ⟵

After grilling, turn your gas grill to high heat and close the lid to help burn off residue. About 5 minutes should do it. Don't forget to turn the gas grill off! After you finish grilling on a charcoal grill, place the lid on it to help burn off the residue. There are plenty of tools that will help, too.

A stiff wire brush with a scraper makes cleaning the grill easy. Tackle this while the grill is still warm.

Crumpled aluminum foil is also a good scraper for the grill grates. Shape it into a loose ball and use long-handled tongs to push it across the grill grates to release the residue.

Natural-bristle basting brushes can be used to apply oil to the grill and baste food during grilling or smoking. (Use separate brushes for oiling grates and basting food.)

Grate Chef Grill Wipes are small pads saturated with high-temperature cooking oil. You can use them for oiling the grill grates prior to cooking, then turn them over to clean the grill when you're finished cooking. The high-temperature oil doesn't smoke, and it doesn't drip from the pads, which prevents flare-ups.

LIGHTING THE FIRE

CHARCOAL GRILLS

A charcoal fire can be started in any of several safe, ecologically sound ways. We prefer using real hardwood lump charcoal instead of compressed charcoal briquettes. It is readily available at most barbecue and grill shops, hardware stores, and some grocery stores. It gives a better flavor and is an all-natural product without chemical additives. It also burns hotter, which is desirable for high-heat grilling.

You can start your hardwood lump charcoal in a metal charcoal chimney or with an electric fire starter, both available at hardware, barbecue, and many gourmet kitchen shops.

Lighting the fire with a charcoal chimney. It is easy to start a charcoal grill with just a match, newspaper, and charcoal. The only special equipment you need is an upright cylindrical metal canister, which looks like a large metal coffee can with a handle. Fill it with fifteen to twenty pieces of hardwood lump charcoal and then place it on a nonflammable surface, such as concrete, gravel, or the grill rack. Slightly tip the chimney to a slant and stuff one or two crumpled sheets of newspaper in the convex-shaped bottom. Light the paper with a match. After 5 minutes, check to make sure that the charcoal has caught fire, or you may need to light another piece of newspaper under the chimney again.

It takes about 15 to 20 minutes for the coals to flame. When the flames subside and the coals are glowing red and just beginning to ash over, it's time to carefully pour the coals onto the fire grates. You can add more charcoal to the fire if you need to, but wait until the new charcoal has begun to ash over before cooking. Start a charcoal grill about 20 to 30 minutes before you're ready to grill.

Lighting the fire with electricity. An electric fire starter is another easy way to start a fire in a charcoal grill. You'll need an outdoor electrical outlet or extension cord. Place the coil on the fire rack of the grill and stack charcoal on top of it. Plug it in, and the fire will start in about 10 to 15 minutes. Remove the coil and let the starter cool on a nonflammable surface, out of the reach of children and pets.

Preparing a direct fire. In this book, when we tell you to "prepare a medium-hot or hot fire in your grill," this means direct heat, with the flames under the food you're cooking.

To create "direct fire," make sure the bottom vents of the grill are open, as fire needs oxygen. Next, start a fire in a charcoal chimney using hardwood lump charcoal and newspaper or using an electric fire starter. Place more hardwood charcoal in the bottom of the grill. When the coals are hot in the charcoal chimney, dump them on top of the charcoal in the bottom of the grill and wait for all the coals to catch fire and ash over. Your fire should extend out about 2 inches (5 cm) beyond the space you will need for the food you plan to grill. When the coals have just begun to ash over and turn a whitish gray, replace the grill grate. Place the food on the grill grate, directly over the coals.

Preparing an indirect fire. When we tell you to "prepare a medium-hot or hot indirect fire in your grill," this means heat on one side of the grill and no heat on the other side.

Prepare a direct fire first, as previously instructed. Once your hot coals are in the bottom of the grill, there are two ways you can create an indirect fire. First, using a long-handled grill spatula, push the coals over to one side of the grill to provide direct heat there. The other side of the grill will now have indirect heat. Second, bank the coals on both sides of the grill. The center of the grill will then be the indirect cooking area. Place the hardwood chunks, chips, or pellets (for wood-smoke flavoring) on top of the coals. Replace the grill grate.

With an indirect fire, you can grill directly over the hot coals while you smoke over the indirect side. When cooking indi-rectly, close the grill lid and use the vents on the top and bottom of the grill to adjust the fire temperature. Open vents allow more oxygen in and make the fire hotter, partially closed vents lower the heat, and closed vents extinguish the fire.

GAS GRILLS

Lighting the gas grill. Follow the manufacturer's directions for starting your gas grill. The manufacturer's directions will tell you how long your grill takes to reach the temperature you want. Newer grills have inset thermometers that register the temperature inside the grill.

Preparing a direct fire. Turn the burners on. Place the food on the grill grate directly over the hot burner: that is direct heat.

Preparing an indirect fire. Your grill must have at least two burners for indirect grilling, preferably side-by-side burners. Fire up the burner on one half of the grill only. The side of the grill with the burner off is for indirect cooking or for quickly moving food off the heat. If you have three or more burners, you may also set up your grill with the two outer burners on and the center of your grill used for indirect cooking. Adjust the burners to regulate the level of heat.

GRILL WITH THE LID OPEN OR SHUT?

Traditionally, grilling was done over an open fire or flame. For some recipes in this book, you'll grill with the lid open. When it is raining or snowing, closing the lid is preferable. Closing the lid allows you to build up more heat, get more wood-smoke flavor in the food, or grill-roast. This will essentially turn the hot grill into a hot oven, meaning your food will cook faster.

GRILLING TEMPERATURE

Most food is grilled over a medium-hot to hot fire, depending on the distance your grill rack sits from the fire and the heat of the fire itself.

In a charcoal grill, the fire is ready when the flames have subsided and the coals are glowing red and just beginning to ash over. This is a hot fire. You can recognize a medium-hot fire when the coals are no longer red but instead are ashen.

For a gas grill, read the manufacturer's directions for the time it takes the grill to reach the desired temperature. Or use a grill thermometer to judge the grill's temperature.

ADJUSTING YOUR GRILL'S TEMPERATURE

On a charcoal grill, always begin the fire with the bottom or side vents open. Lower the temperature by partially closing the vents, and raise the temperature by opening the vents or by adding more charcoal to ratchet up the fire. More air means the fire will burn faster and hotter; less air makes for a slower and lower-temperature fire.

On a gas grill, adjust the heat by turning the heat-control knobs to the desired level. Most heat-control knobs are marked "high," "medium," and "low," although some are marked only "high" and "low." On some models, you can control the specific temperature by turning the temperature dial.

HOW TO GRILL

Once your grill is at the proper temperature, follow our recipe directions for grilling. Good grill marks are desirable and accomplished by searing and charring before turning the food with grill tongs or a grill spatula. Avoid turning the food too early. The food needs to sit undisturbed for a time to get those lovely grill marks.

To wood grill, you need to either start with an all-wood fire or add wood to a charcoal or gas fire, and then grill with the lid open. With wood grilling, you will get a hot, aromatic fire that will give your foods a bit of char and just a hint of smoke, less than a "kiss of smoke" and much less than slow smoking. Wood grilling usually means a hotter fire and grilling with the lid open. It's a popular technique in restaurants around the country, but easily achievable in your backyard.

If you want to wood grill in a fireplace or fire pit, build a wood fire using hardwoods (not pine). You can simply do a little yard work, like we do, and gather enough oak, maple, hickory, alder, pecan, apple, cherry, or black walnut wood, depending on where you live. You can also purchase wood chunks to add to the fire. Arrange the grill grate and start the fire. When the coals are ashed over, your fire is hot and aromatic enough for you to start grilling.

In a charcoal grill, ignite the charcoal. When the charcoal has ashed over, add a few sticks of your favorite hardwood to the coals. When the wood flames up, you can start to grill.

In a gas grill, add dry wood chips or pellets to the smoker box. You could also create a foil packet of pellets or chips and poke holes in it to let the smoke escape. Place the smoker box or foil packet near or over the hottest part of the grill. When you see the first wisp of smoke, you can start to grill.

HOW TO GRILL WITH A KISS OF SMOKE

You can give your food more of the aroma of wood smoke when you use this technique. Basically, you add wood to the fire and grill with the lid closed.

On a charcoal grill, you could add small, seasoned branches of hardwoods like oak, maple, or pecan; fruitwoods like apple, pear, or peach; or even dried grapevines or woody herb stalks like rosemary or lavender. You simply add a branch or two, several wood chunks, or a handful of wood chips to the fire after the coals have ashed over.

You want to wait to put your food on until you see the first wisp of smoke (so you know the wood is smoldering and you'll get the wood-smoke flavor you want). Then simply place your food on the grill grate, close the lid, and let the food smoke and grill at the same time.

For a gas grill, you want to avoid any debris getting into the gas jets, so you'll want to contain the wood in a homemade aluminum foil packet or in a metal smoker box you can buy at barbecue shops, gourmet stores with barbecue accessories, or hardware stores. We find that dry wood chips smolder more quickly, so simply place a large handful or about 1 cup (55 g) of fine wood chips or wood pellets (available at kitchen, barbecue, or hardware stores that carry barbecue accessories) in an aluminum foil packet or metal smoker box. If using foil, poke holes in the packet.

Place the packet or smoker box close to a fired gas jet, using grill tongs. When you see the first wisp of smoke, simply place your food on the grill grate, close the lid, and let the food smoke and grill at the same time.

The wood chips or pellets will smolder rather than burn, adding smoky flavor for about 1 hour.

HOW TO SLOW SMOKE

In parts of America—the Carolinas, Georgia, Tennessee, Missouri, Kansas, Oklahoma, and Texas—slow smoking is the same as barbecuing, as in "Are you barbecuing that pork butt?"

Slow smoking means cooking your food at lower temperatures, over a long period of time, with the aroma of smoldering wood and the lid closed. Here's how you do it:

Use regional wood. These are chunks of seasoned hardwood packaged in bags and available at grocery, barbecue, and hardware stores. These larger chunks smolder more slowly to flavor foods that need hours to get a smoky flavor. Barbecuers generally use what is available in their area. To understand the characteristics of regional woods, see American Woods for Grilling and Smoking (page 23).

Go low. To cook at 225°F/107°C to 250°F/121°C, the food needs to be at a distance from the fire. Bullet-shaped smokers are designed to do this for you, with the fire in the bottom and the food on the top tier. You can also create an indirect fire in your grill, with a fire on one side and no fire on the other. You put your food on the no-fire side.

Go slow. As in hours, not minutes. For a charcoal grill, prepare an indirect fire in your grill, with a fire on one side and no fire on the other. Simply place the wood chunks on the ashen coals. When you see the first wisp of smoke, put the food on the no-fire side, close the lid, and start to slow smoke. Replenish the charcoal and wood as needed for additional fire and smoke.

For a gas grill, prepare an indirect fire in your grill, with a fire on one side and no fire on the other. Place the wood chips or wood pellets in a foil packet, poke holes in the top to let the smoke out, and place the packet near a burner so the wood will smolder. When you see the first wisp of smoke, put the food on the no-fire side, close the lid,

and start to slow smoke. Replenish the wood chip packets as needed for additional smoke.

Moisturize. For foods that take a long time to slow smoke, such as brisket and pork butt or shoulder, you need to spray the meat with a flavorful liquid or baste it from time to time. Each recipe will tell you what liquid to use and when to spray or baste to keep the meat from drying out.

HOW TO SLOW SMOKE VEGETABLES, FRUITS, AND NUTS

Smoking fresh foods that don't need to be "done" is simplicity itself. It's one of those fairly effortless ways to ratchet up the flavor—without adding fat grams or carbs.

If you're going to set up your grill or your smoker, why not think ahead and smoke several things at a time? Just place the foods to be smoked in separate disposable aluminum pans. Use whatever woods you like, except for heavier woods like hickory and mesquite, which could be too smoky. Try alder, apple, cherry, maple, oak, pecan, or a combination.

Place the pans of food on the smoker. Cover and smoke at 225°F to 250°F (107°C to 121°C). Let them smoke for about an hour, or until they're bronzed and have a smoky aroma. That's it. Remember: Vegetables, fruits, and nuts don't have to be done; you just want them to be smoky.

You can enjoy your smoked goodies right away, cover and refrigerate them for a day or two, or wrap and freeze them for up to 3 months.

Here are the best candidates for slow smoking:

Bell or chile peppers: Core, halve, and seed each pepper. Brush with olive oil and smoke for 1 hour, or until soft and aromatic.

Garlic: Slice about $1/2$ inch (1.3 cm) off the top and bottom of whole heads of garlic. Place them larger side–down in the pan and drizzle with olive oil. Smoke for 1 to $1^1/_2$ hours, or until soft when you squeeze the bulb. Squeeze the garlic pulp out of each head.

Onions: Peel and slice onions, place in the pan, and drizzle with olive oil. Smoke for 30 to 40 minutes, or until soft and aromatic.

Orchard fruits: Peel, core, and quarter apples, pears, peaches, nectarines, and plums and smoke for 1 hour, or until aromatic.

Tomatoes: Use four large beefsteak tomatoes, cored, or twelve Roma tomatoes, cut in half lengthwise, and smoke for 1 hour, or until aromatic.

Potatoes or sweet potatoes: Using a carving fork, poke holes in the potatoes. Set on the indirect side of a grill and smoke for about $1^1/_2$ hours, or until a fork can easily be inserted into the potato.

Winter squash: Halve and seed acorn or butternut squash or pumpkins. Cover the cut side of the squash with foil and poke holes in the foil to let the smoke through. Smoke cut-side down for about 1 hour, or until the meat of the squash is tender.

Tree nuts: Smoke shelled almonds, cashews, and pecans for 1 hour, or until aromatic. The nuts will soften. If you want them crisp again, place the smoked nuts on a baking sheet in a 350°F (177°C) oven for 15 minutes, or until toasty.

HOW TO PLANK

Planking involves simply placing food on a seasoned, untreated, aromatic wood plank and then cooking it on the grill with the lid closed. You can buy wood planks for the oven or for the grill at kitchen, hardware, barbecue, or online stores. The most commonly used planks are rectangular and vary slightly in size. Grilling planks are thin and range in size from about 12 x $1/2$ to $3/_4$ inches (30 x 1.3 to 1.9 cm). Oven planks are thick and have a concave oval that holds sauces on the plank. They are most common in cedar (which is a wider plank, about $9^1/_2$ x 15 x $1^1/_2$ inches/24 x 38 x 3.8 cm) or alder. Oven planks are more expensive, so you want to make sure they don't char too much, and then they will last longer. Use whatever size fits best on your grill. Food cooks in about the same time on thinner or thicker planks, but thicker planks last longer. Planks can be reused until they're either too charred or too brittle to hold food.

Although planking on cedar is the universal favorite, as it gives the best aromatic flavor, any regional hardwood—such as alder, hickory, maple, oak, mesquite, apple, or cherry—will produce great-tasting planked food, too. A simple test is to sniff the plank. If you can't smell any aromatic wood, it's not going to impart flavor to your food. Go for the plank with the best aroma.

To use the plank, submerge it in water for at least an hour. A deep sink and a large rectangular plastic container that you can fill with water both work. Use a couple of large cans to weigh down the plank so that it stays under the surface. A water-soaked plank produces maximum smoke flavor and is more resistant to charring on the grill.

Prepare an indirect (medium-hot or hot on one side, no heat on the other) fire in your grill. You can do this with a gas grill with dual burners or in a charcoal grill by massing the hot coals on the "hot" side. For wider charcoal grills or gas grills with three burners, you can make the indirect part in the middle, with coals or lit burners on each side.

The food surface that touches the wood plank takes on more flavor, so don't crowd the food onto the plank. Use two planks, if necessary. Then close the grill lid and cook according to the time specified in the recipe. Stay close by, though, in case of flare-ups. Keep a spray bottle filled with water handy, just in case.

For a rustic bistro effect, serve the food right on the plank, like a platter. After you've cooked and served on the plank, clean it up with a little hot, soapy water and a good rinse. (*Do not soak* the plank in soapy water.) Eighty-grit sandpaper may be used to help clean the plank, too. Let it air-dry and store in a cupboard uncovered.

⟶ HARDWOOD FLAVORS FOR PLANKING ⟵

Alder gives a light, aromatic flavor and is great paired with fish.

Cedar is probably the most aromatic of the woods, lending a deep but gentle woodsy flavor to planked foods of all kinds.

Hickory lends a stronger, hearty wood flavor to beef, pork, and poultry.

Maple smolders to a sweeter, milder flavor that pairs well with poultry, vegetables, and fish.

Oak gives a medium, woodsy aroma without being bitter. It pairs well with any food.

CAST-IRON GRILLING

Cast-iron griddles or skillets, heated to a high temperature on the grill, can sear great steaks, fish fillets, or shellfish like scallops or shrimp.

First, heat the griddle or skillet with the grill lid closed for about 20 minutes, or until it is very hot and the inside bottom of the skillet is starting to turn a grayish color.

Brush the steak on both sides with oil and grill on the griddle or in the skillet, uncovered, for 2 to 3 minutes per side, turning once for a black and bleu steak that is charry on the outside and rare in the center. Grill longer on each side, if you wish, for a steak that is done to your liking.

For fish, brush both sides of the fish fillet with oil, place on the griddle or in the skillet, close the grill lid, and grill for 3 to 4 minutes, turning once, or until the fish begins to flake when tested with a fork in the thickest part.

For shellfish, brush both sides of the scallops or shrimp with oil, place on the griddle or in the skillet, close the grill lid, and grill for 2 minutes per side, turning once, or until the shellfish just begins to turn opaque and is firm. Shellfish keeps cooking in residual heat, so take it off the griddle or out of the skillet immediately.

WHEN IS YOUR FOOD DONE ON THE GRILL?

Vegetables, breads, sandwiches, and fruits are done when they have good grill marks or they're tender enough for your liking. Easy.

We recommend that if you're just starting to grill, you use an instant-read meat thermometer to test the doneness of grilled breads and meats: chicken, pork, beef, veal, game, and lamb. Insert the thermometer into the thickest part of the meat or bread and read the temperature. After a while, you'll be able to tell the doneness of grilled foods by look, smell, and touch. When you touch a pork or beef tenderloin with tongs and it's soft and wiggly, it's too rare. When the tenderloin begins to offer some resistance, it's rare to medium-rare. When it just begins to firm up, it's medium. When it feels solid, it's well-done. For exact temperatures and a great guide to knowing when meat is cooked, please use the handy chart on page 22.

DONENESS CHART FOR GRILLING

Personal preferences run the gamut from very rare to very well-done.
Use this chart as a guideline for your outdoor grilling.

Sandwiches	Good grill marks and an internal temperature of 150°F/66°C, when cheese starts to melt
Bread	Good grill marks
Vegetables	Good grill marks and done to your liking
Fruits	Good grill marks and done to your liking
Beef	125°F/52°C for rare, 140°F/60°C for medium, 160°F/71°C for well-done
Chicken breast	160°F/71°C
Turkey breast	165°F/74°C
Fish fillet	Begins to flake when tested with a fork in thickest part
Shellfish	Opaque and somewhat firm to the touch
Lamb	125°F/52°C for rare, 140°F/60°C for medium
Pork	140°F/60°C for medium, 160°F/71°C for well-done

GRILLING ON SKEWERS

For grilling foods on skewers, you can use wood or bamboo skewers, campfire sticks (that you pick up in your yard), fresh rosemary or lavender herb branches, or metal skewers. Wood or bamboo skewers, which come in packages at the grocery store, need to be soaked in water for at least 30 minutes before threading them with food and grilling. After grilling, just throw the charred skewers away.

STIR-GRILLING

Stir-grilling foods over a hot fire is a great way to show off your vegetable harvest—and there's no mess in the kitchen!

To stir-grill, you need a grill wok or basket (a hexagonal metal wok or round basket with perforations), along with wooden spoons, paddles, or long-handled spatulas. The perforations in the wok or basket allow for more of the grill flavors to penetrate the food. Grill woks are usually 12 to 15 inches (30 to 38 cm) in size. We prefer a bigger wok because more space means potentially more grill flavor and more room for a larger quantity of food. We like to use long-handled wooden paddles or spoons to toss the food in a grill wok. We call this technique "stir-grilling," a similar but healthier alternative to stir-frying.

So roll up your sleeves, take a deep breath, and get ready to rumble on out to the grill, where great food is your manifest destiny!

AMERICAN WOODS FOR GRILLING AND SMOKING

American hardwoods can give a true taste of place. From maple in the East to red oak in the West, you can use many seasoned hardwoods for wood grilling, grilling with a kiss of smoke, and slow smoking. You want wood that is as natural as possible, not treated with chemicals. We usually just do a little yard work and can pick up enough sticks for wood grilling or grilling with a kiss of smoke. For slow smoking, you can buy regional wood (in pellets, chips, chunks, sticks, and logs) from online sources like Chigger Creek Wood Products, Carolina Cookwood, Fruita Wood, and Woodyard BBQ or from a hardware store near you.

Acacia. Smoke similar to mesquite for smoking brisket.

Alder. Stately trees from the Northwest with pale wood that offers a delicate aroma. Good with fish, pork, poultry, and light-meat game birds.

Almond. From California, this wood has a sweeter smoke flavor that is good with chicken, pork, fish, vegetables, and fruit.

Apple. Sweetly aromatic, this fragrant wood from the Midwest and Northeast is good with poultry, pork, fruit, and vegetables.

Cherry. From the Midwest, cherry burns well and produces a medium, fruity smoke that darkens foods. Good with beef and pork.

Corn cobs. Dried corn cobs, corn kernels removed, produce a sweet smoke and give foods a golden appearance. We've used them on shrimp, chicken, and pork.

English and black walnut. Walnut trees proliferate from the Midwest to California, yet you rarely hear of anyone using the wood for grilling or smoking. Walnut trees tend to shed nuts rather than sticks, so that might be part of the reason. The other is that walnut produces a heavier smoke, so it is best used with other woods for slow smoking.

Grapevines. The prunings from any grape-producing region afford a piquant smoke good for wood grilling or grilling with a kiss of smoke.

Hickory. Comes from the South and Midwest. Good, as you might guess, with anything you'd like to slow smoke, from vegetables to game. It is a heavier wood smoke, so use it in moderation or in combination with lighter-flavored woods.

Maple. A wood synonymous with New England, maple has a mellow flavor good for grilling or slow smoking vegetables, chicken, beef, or pork.

Mesquite. More of a bush than a tree, the gnarly mesquite grows in arid regions of the Southwest. It burns hot for wood grilling and gives a heavy smoke for slow smoking. Use it in moderation.

Nut shells. Dry shells from hazelnuts and pecans, smashed into tiny pieces, can also smolder to a medium smoke for food flavor on cheese or seafood.

Oak. All oak varieties—including red oak from California, post oak from Texas, white oak from Ohio, pin oak from Missouri, and many more—do well for wood grilling and slow smoking. Oak burns for a longer time than other woods and has a medium-heavy smoke that is good for all kinds of foods, but use in moderation.

Peach, Nectarine, and Apricot. Yes, you can grill and smoke with these fruitwoods, too. The late, great Karen Putman, who won every major barbecue award, loved peach wood smoke with pork because its flavor is milder than hickory.

Pear. From the Northeast and the Pacific Northwest, seasoned pear wood burns like other fruitwood and has a more delicate smoke flavor that is good with fruit, vegetables, fish, poultry, and lamb.

Pecan. Pecan trees grow wild in Midwestern groves and are cultivated in the South. Pecan wood is good for wood grilling, as it gives a steady, aromatic heat. It's also good for slow smoking, with a medium flavor, delicious with cheese, vegetables, and meats.

CHAPTER ONE

Happy Hour
Drinks, Small Plates,
and Snacks

WE MIGHT HAVE THE UNITED STATES NAVY TO THANK FOR the concept of happy hour.

Taking cues since the 1880s from their wives' "happy hour social clubs," which may or may not have involved alcohol, Navy men officially went in for happy hour on the U.S.S. *Arkansas* in 1913, then went all out for happy hours after World War I.

The idea of a cocktail hour before dinner gained wider appeal after drinking alcohol was banned during Prohibition (1920–33) and people thrilled to the idea of sneaking into speakeasies.

Today, happy hour means a social time of small plates and little bites with or without beer, wine, or cocktails. You can make a meal on happy hour food, if it's done right. And if it's delicious.

In this chapter, we start out with a colorful showstopper—Burrata-Stuffed Squash Blossoms with Tapenade (page 26). With grilled bread, this appetizer goes garden-to-grill-to-table. If you eat with your eyes as well as your taste buds, this is a feast.

We reinvent the chip-and-dip with delicious farm-fresh goodies to grill and serve with a sauce for dipping. Try Grilled Baby Artichokes with Blood Orange Drizzle (page 30) and Grilled Rainbow Carrot Fries with Roasted Pepper Ketchup (page 46). Snacking gets a delicious makeover with Big Easy Blackened Okra (page 32), Smoke-Roasted Sweet Potatoes with Spicy-Sweet Sorghum Butter (page 34), and Grilled Fava Beans with Pecorino (page 31).

We whip up a batch of cocktails that taste even better with a hint of grill marks and a wisp of smoke.

And we serve up slightly heartier fare that is still perfect for sharing: Grilled Chicken Skewers with Strawberry Rhubarb BBQ Sauce (page 44) and Cedar-Planked Charcuterie (page 33).

Are we happy yet?

Burrata-Stuffed Squash Blossoms with Tapenade

Blistered Shishito Peppers
on Grilled Bread with Ricotta

Grilled Baby Artichokes
with Blood Orange Drizzle

Grilled Fava Beans with Pecorino

Big Easy Blackened Okra

Cedar-Planked Charcuterie with Pickled Beets

Smoke-Roasted Sweet Potatoes
with Spicy-Sweet Sorghum Butter

Smoked Salmon Spread

Artichoke–Red Pepper Spread

Tomato-Avocado Relish

Wood-Grilled Oysters with Two Smoky Sauces

Cajun Grilled Gulf Shrimp
with Horseradish Cream Sauce

Pecan-Smoked Goat Cheese Stuffed Peppadews

Grilled Chicken Skewers with
Strawberry Rhubarb BBQ Sauce

Grilled Rainbow Carrot Fries
with Roasted Pepper "Ketchup"

Grilled Lemon Whiskey Sour

Grilled Persimmon and Smoked Thyme Cocktail

Smoked Bloody Mary with Bacon

Grilled Fruit Sangria

BURRATA-STUFFED
SQUASH BLOSSOMS *with* TAPENADE

When squash blossoms are available in your area, try this easy dish, adapted from one that Melissa Clark featured in the New York Times. *You'll need a perforated grill rack or a round metal pizza pan that can go from grill to table. Hot off the grill, this looks like a vivid abstract expressionist painting—check out the work of Jackson Pollock. Just use a fork to gently slide a squash blossom or two, along with the deliciously oozing burrata and black olive tapenade, onto a slice of grilled bread.*

Serves 4

BLACK OLIVE TAPENADE

1 cup (125 g) thinly sliced cured black olives

2 tablespoons (25 ml) olive oil

Grated zest and juice of 1 lemon

2 tablespoons (28 g) unsalted butter, at room temperature

SQUASH BLOSSOMS

12 fresh squash blossoms

8 ounces (227 g) burrata or fresh buffalo mozzarella

Olive oil

Kosher salt and freshly ground black pepper

8 slices Italian or French country bread

For the Black Olive Tapenade, combine the olives, olive oil, lemon zest, lemon juice, and butter in a bowl. Use right away or store, covered, in the refrigerator for up to 3 days before serving.

Prepare a medium-hot fire in your grill. Slice one side of each squash blossom from blossom end to base so you can stuff it with a finger-sized (about 1 table-spoon/15 g) piece of burrata. Oil a perforated grill rack or a round metal pizza pan. Arrange the stuffed squash blossoms on the pan, sliced-side up, and dot them in the center with tapenade. Brush each squash blossom with olive oil and season with salt and pepper. Brush each slice of country bread with olive oil.

Grill the bread for 1 minute or so on each side, or until it has good grill marks. Keep warm. Place the pan of stuffed squash blossoms on the grill. Close the lid and grill for 2 to 4 minutes, not turning, or until the burrata oozes and the squash blossoms are slightly browned. Serve from the pan with grilled bread and extra tapenade on the side.

BLISTERED SHISHITO PEPPERS ON GRILLED BREAD *with* RICOTTA

We both grow these bushy peppers in our Kansas City gardens, so we can just go out and pick a bunch when we like. When they start to produce in mid-summer, these small, mild green peppers go straight on the grill. Although Japanese cooks poke a little hole in the base of the pepper to keep it from puffing up, we don't. A brush of olive oil, a sprinkling of salt and pepper, and they grill and puff up to addictive deliciousness. We've had them as a snack (in a cast-iron skillet with melted Monterey Jack cheese at Empellón Taqueria in New York City) and as a side dish with roast chicken (at The Girl and the Goat in Chicago). Serve these atop grilled bread spread with fresh ricotta from a local dairy and a drizzle of olive oil. Other peppers may be substituted for the shishitos, like sweet banana, sweet mini peppers, or sweet yellow or cubanelles.

Serves 4

16 shishito peppers
4 slices artisan country bread
Olive oil
Kosher salt and freshly ground
  black pepper
1 cup (227 g) fresh ricotta

Prepare a medium-hot fire in your grill.

Brush the peppers and bread slices with olive oil. Sprinkle the peppers with salt and pepper.

Grill the bread slices for about 1 minute per side, or until they have good grill marks. Place the peppers perpendicular to the grill grates and grill for about 2 minutes per side, or until the peppers have puffed up and are slightly charry.

Spread one side of each bread slice with a fourth of the ricotta and top with 4 peppers. Drizzle with a little more olive oil and serve.

GRILLED BABY ARTICHOKES
with BLOOD ORANGE DRIZZLE

Tender baby artichokes herald the beginning of fine weather and are delicious on the grill. You can grow artichokes in your garden, or be glad for Castroville in central California. Founded by Juan Bautista Castro (Spaniards were credited with bringing the artichoke to California), Castroville was ringed with wetlands until they were drained and converted to farmland by Chinese workers in the 1860s. By 1923, there were nine artichoke growers. Today, Castroville is the Artichoke Capital of the United States. Blood oranges, also grown in California, are just ending their season as artichokes come in—like two delicious ships passing in the night. You might also want to use a California olive oil, such as that from California Olive Ranch.

Serves 4

8 baby artichokes

Grated zest and juice of 1 lemon

1/2 teaspoon kosher salt, plus more for seasoning

1 garlic clove, minced

Grated zest and juice of 1 blood or navel orange

1/2 cup (120 ml) olive oil

Freshly ground black pepper

Remove the bottom outer leaves from the artichokes and trim off the stems. Slice the artichokes in half lengthwise. Trim about 1 inch (2.5 cm) off the tips. Snip a little off the tops of each of the remaining outer leaves. With the tip of a teaspoon, remove the hairy chokes and discard.

In a large, nonreactive pot, bring 1 inch (2.5 cm) of water, the lemon zest, lemon juice, and salt to a boil over medium-high heat. Add the artichokes, cover, and cook for 5 to 6 minutes, or until the artichoke bottoms are tender when pierced with a small knife. Drain well and set aside.

Prepare a medium-hot fire in your grill.

In a small bowl, whisk the garlic, orange zest, orange juice, and olive oil together. Add salt and pepper to taste. Brush the artichokes with some of the vinaigrette.

Grill the artichokes for 5 minutes, turning frequently, until the exterior is slightly charry. Serve hot or at room temperature with the remaining Blood Orange Drizzle.

GRILLED FAVA BEANS
with PECORINO

When we taught a grilling class in Napa, California, we picked fava beans from the garden a mere hour before we fired up the grill. Fava beans grow in long pods, like shell beans or sugar snap peas, and you can grill them in the pod for a bit of smoky flavor and to retain the crunch of the bean. These are wonderful with fresh and crumbly pecorino rather than an aged one better for grating. They are also good as a vegan option dipped in Smoked Cashew Crema (page 72). If you want to grow fava beans in your garden, check out Seeds from Italy (growitalian.com), based—improbably—near us in Lawrence, Kansas.

Serves 4

1 pound (454 g) fava beans
  in the pod
Olive oil
Kosher salt and freshly ground
  black pepper
8 ounces (227 g) fresh pecorino,
  crumbled

Prepare a medium-hot fire in your grill.

Brush the beans with olive oil and sprinkle with salt and pepper.

Grill the beans, turning often, for 10 to 12 minutes, or until the pods have good grill marks.

To serve, arrange the fava bean pods on a platter and pass a bowl of crumbled pecorino. Offer each guest a plate. Try eating the fava beans, pod and all, with a little pecorino and a drizzle of olive oil. If the pods are too tough, squeeze out the fava beans and eat them with the cheese and olive oil.

BIG EASY BLACKENED OKRA

Oh, my! Okra is a standout in the garden, a tall branching plant with eye-catching flowers. If you've never had okra grilled before, you're in for a treat. With a brush of olive oil and a sprinkle of Cajun seasoning, they have the flavor of Paul Prudhomme's classic blackened dishes, minus the roux and butter. Thread four on a skewer and then grill on both sides. Then fight over who gets to eat them. With a cold beer on a hot summer night, nothin' finer. Make up this Blackening Spice Rub or buy your favorite readymade Cajun spice mixture.

Serves 4 to 6

BLACKENING SPICE RUB

1 tablespoon Hungarian paprika

1 tablespoon kosher salt

1 tablespoon garlic powder

1½ teaspoons freshly ground black pepper

1½ teaspoons onion powder

1½ teaspoons dried oregano

1½ teaspoons dried thyme

1 teaspoon cayenne pepper

OKRA

48 fresh okra pods (about 1½ pounds/680 g)

Olive oil

Prepare a hot fire in your grill. Soak 12 (12-inch/30 cm) bamboo skewers in water for 30 minutes.

For the Blackening Spice Rub: Combine all the spice mix ingredients.

Thread four okra pods horizontally on each skewer, piercing through the center of each pod. Brush the skewers with olive oil and season generously on both sides with the blackening spice.

Oil the grill grates and then place the skewers on the grates. Grill for 2 to 3 minutes on each side, or until the okra blisters and begins to blacken.

To serve, slide the okra pods off each skewer and pile on a platter.

CEDAR-PLANKED CHARCUTERIE
with PICKLED BEETS

Charcuterie was once the province of the mom-and-pop butcher shop. When those started to fade away, chefs took up the slack. In the college town of Lawrence, Kansas, two restaurants make their own sausage and preserved meats. The restaurant 715 specializes in Italian-style coppa and sausage, while Hank Charcuterie goes in for more heavily smoked kielbasa, bacon, and duck breast. If you have really good charcuterie in your area, enjoy it as it is or slightly warmed, as in this recipe. The more the surface of the meat or cheese touches the plank, the more gentle aromatic flavor of the cedar it will get. The tops of the meat and cheese will get the gentle flavor of the grill and slightly soften to bring out their flavors. If you can't make your own charcuterie, you can still make the pickled beets, which taste good with just about anything.

Serves 6 to 8

PICKLED BEETS

1 (15-ounce/425 g) can sliced beets or 4 fresh cooked and peeled beets, sliced

1 medium-size red onion, sliced

3/4 cup (180 ml) white vinegar

3/4 cup (180 ml) water

1/4 cup (68 g) granulated sugar

1 tablespoon kosher salt

CHARCUTERIE

1 (6-ounce/170 g) wedge blue cheese

1 (6-ounce/170 g) wedge Fontina cheese

1 (6-ounce/170 g) wedge Gouda cheese

16 slices coppa or salami

Crusty bread or crisp crackers

Assorted mustards

For the Pickled Beets, in a quart (1 L) jar with a wide mouth, alternate layers of sliced beets and sliced red onion.

In a large bowl, combine the vinegar, water, sugar, and salt. Stir until the sugar and salt have dissolved. Pour the liquid into the jar to just cover the beets and onions. Cover with the lid and keep refrigerated for up to a couple of weeks. Beets need at least 8 hours to "pickle."

Submerge a cedar oven plank in water for at least 1 hour.

Prepare an indirect fire in your grill, with a hot fire on one side and no fire on the other (see How to Plank, page 19).

Arrange the cheeses and meats on the plank.

Place the plank on the indirect, no-heat side and close the lid. Plank cook for 15 to 20 minutes, or until the cheese has started to melt slightly. Serve from the plank with a basket of bread or crackers, assorted mustards, and Pickled Beets.

SMOKE-ROASTED SWEET POTATOES
with SPICY-SWEET SORGHUM BUTTER

Baby sweet potatoes are a real treat, usually available in late summer or early fall at Coon Rock Farm in Hillsborough, North Carolina, or at a farmers' market near you. But you can cut large sweet potatoes down to fingerling size and still have delicious finger food. You can also substitute white or purple fingerling potatoes in this recipe. It's a blueprint, after all, for your creativity. Dipped in a spicy butter sweetened with sorghum, a syrup made from a grass that is enjoying a comeback, they're divine. A little time on the smoker (we suggest using hickory, pecan, or oak wood), a little time in the oven, and sweet potatoes have a smoky flavor with a crispy finish.

Serves 4

SPICY-SWEET SORGHUM BUTTER

4 ounces (113 g) unsalted butter, at room temperature

1 small red chile, stemmed, seeded, and diced

½ teaspoon freshly grated orange zest

2 tablespoons sorghum syrup or maple syrup

¼ teaspoon freshly grated nutmeg

Kosher salt

SMOKE-ROASTED SWEET POTATOES

2 pounds (1 kg) fingerling sweet potatoes or sweet potatoes cut into fingerling size

Olive oil

Kosher salt and freshly ground black pepper

For the Spicy-Sweet Sorghum Butter, mash the butter, red chile, orange zest, sorghum, and nutmeg together in a medium bowl. Season with salt.

Prepare a medium-hot indirect fire in your grill or smoker with hickory, pecan, or oak wood (see How to Slow Smoke, page 17). In an aluminum pan, toss the fingerlings with olive oil to coat, and then season with salt and pepper. Smoke at 250°F (121°C) for 1 hour, or until the potatoes are burnished and have a smoky aroma. Meanwhile, preheat your indoor oven to 450°F (232°C).

Transfer the potatoes to the hot oven and roast for 20 minutes, or until tender and slightly crispy.

To serve, place the butter in a bowl in the middle of a platter and surround with the luscious fingerlings.

⟶ SORGHUM: A TASTE OF PLACE ⟵

Two kinds of sorghum are grown in grassy areas of the Midwest and the South. Grain sorghum was traditionally grown for animal feed but has found a new purpose in gluten-free flour. Sweet sorghum is harvested like sugar cane and boiled down to make sorghum syrup, with Tennessee and Kentucky leading the production. Sorghum syrup, like maple syrup or wine, takes on the taste of its terroir, or where it is grown. Flavors can include caramel, spice, citrus, and anise.

- Muddy Pond Sorghum Mill, Monterey, Tennessee: A lighter, molasses-like flavor.
- Oberholtzer's Kentucky Sorghum, Liberty, Kentucky: Warm, caramel flavor.
- Bates County Sorghum, Rich Hill, Missouri: Dark and molasses-like, very rich.
- Gold Run Sorghum, Camden, Indiana: Rich, brown, spicy.
- Maasdam Sorghum Mills, Lynnville, Iowa: Medium-spiced, citrusy.
- Sandhill Sorghum, Rutledge, Missouri: Mild, with a hint of citrus and spice.

GRILLED BREAD
with LOTS OF TOPPINGS

Our friend and acclaimed chef Michael Smith won a James Beard Best Chef of the Midwest award several years ago. His signature restaurant, Michael Smith, in Kansas City is a lovely white-tablecloth place, and next door is his casual, tapas-style Extra-Virgin, which serves the most delicious grilled bread we have ever had. His secret? Great artisan country bread sliced medium thick and grilled over fire for maximum crusty char.

The better the bread, the better it is grilled, so good artisan bread is essential. Ciabatta, country French or Italian, sourdough, rye, baguette, or any other bread with a sturdy crumb will do. Smaller loaves of bread sliced thin are easier for handheld treats, while larger, thicker slices of bread may need to be plated with knife and fork to eat. Buy a loaf of bread and hand-slice it for the thinness or thickness that you desire. Hand-slicing also gives the bread slice a roughed-up surface, perfect for getting extra bits of char. Lightly drizzle or brush olive oil on both sides of the bread and then grill over a hot fire for about 30 to 60 seconds on each side, until the bread has good char or grill marks on it. Serve the bread hot off the grill with toppings. It is also good served at room temperature.

Here is a great list of toppings and recipes to get you started:
- ★ Aioli and grilled shrimp topped with snipped chives
- ★ Aioli and feta cheese topped with chopped pistachios
- ★ Aioli and sliced beef tenderloin topped with shaved pecorino and arugula
- ★ Pesto and thin, sliced grilled chicken topped with bacon crumbles
- ★ Burrata or mozzarella and sliced tomatoes topped with fresh basil or a dollop of pesto
- ★ Goat cheese and orange marmalade or fig preserves topped with crumbled bacon and fresh herbs
- ★ Goat cheese topped with slices of fresh grilled figs or nectarines
- ★ Blue cheese softened and topped with melon, apple, or pear slices and watercress
- ★ Black Olive Tapenade (page 26) topped with sliced tomato
- ★ Beefsteak tomatoes chopped and mixed with capers
- ★ Feta cheese drizzled with honey or topped with fig or cherry preserves
- ★ Avocado sliced or mashed and topped with a spoonful of salsa
- ★ Flavored herb butter topped with slices of hard-cooked egg and red or black caviar
- ★ Fresh ricotta cheese topped with thinly sliced radishes and dill sprigs

SMOKED SALMON SPREAD

Makes about 1¹/₂ cups/354 ml

4 ounces (113 g) smoked or grilled salmon, flaked

8 ounces (227 g) cream cheese, at room temperature

¹/₂ medium-size red onion, finely chopped

2 tablespoons capers

1 tablespoon freshly squeezed lemon juice

Combine all the ingredients, stir to blend, and serve with grilled bread.

★ ★ ★

ARTICHOKE–RED PEPPER SPREAD

Makes 1³/₄ cups/414 ml

¹/₂ cup (84 g) chopped artichoke hearts

¹/₂ cup (56 g) grated Parmesan or Romano cheese

¹/₄ cup (42 g) chopped roasted red peppers

¹/₄ cup (56 g) sour cream

¹/₄ cup (56 g) mayonnaise

Combine all the ingredients, stir to blend, and serve with grilled bread.

★ ★ ★

TOMATO-AVOCADO RELISH

Makes about 2 cups/473 ml

1 pint (310 g) cherry tomatoes, halved

1 large ripe avocado, pitted and diced

2 tablespoons finely chopped red onion

1 jalapeño pepper, seeded and diced

2 garlic cloves, minced

¹/₄ cup (21 g) finely minced fresh flat-leaf parsley

2 tablespoons extra-virgin olive oil

2 tablespoons freshly squeezed lime juice

Kosher salt and freshly ground black pepper

Combine all the ingredients, stir to blend, and serve with grilled bread.

WOOD-GRILLED OYSTERS
with TWO SMOKY SAUCES

Over 150 varieties spring from the five main types of North American oysters: Kumamoto, Pacific, Atlantic, Eastern, and European flats. From Alaska to Baja California and Maine to the Chesapeake Bay, oysters thrive in coastal waters. Like wine that takes on hints of flavor from its terroir or microclimate, oysters take on hints of flavor from their "merroir," or marine environment. They can taste sweet, briny, creamy, herbaceous, mineral-y, and even vegetal. A kiss of smoke (see page 17) gives these bivalves a hint of mystery, and the two smoky sauces carry that theme forward (try alder, apple, hickory, oak, pecan, or mesquite wood for smoking). Keep oysters cold until you grill them. And another tip: Ditch the plastic container or bag when you get home. Put the oysters on the half shell between layers of wet newspaper topped with a wet towel on a tray in the refrigerator and grill within 24 hours.

Serves 6 to 8

SMOKY COCKTAIL SAUCE

1 (11-ounce/312 g) bottle cocktail sauce

1 tablespoon prepared horse-radish, or more to taste

1 teaspoon liquid smoke flavoring

CHIPOTLE-GARLIC-CILANTRO BUTTER

8 ounces (227 g) unsalted butter, melted

4 garlic cloves, minced

Juice of 1 lemon

2 teaspoons chipotle sauce

2 tablespoons finely chopped cilantro leaves

WOOD-GRILLED OYSTERS

24 to 32 fresh oysters, shucked and chilled

Make the Smoky Cocktail Sauce and the Chipotle-Garlic-Cilantro Butter. In a small bowl, whisk the cocktail sauce, horseradish, and liquid smoke flavoring together until well blended. In a separate bowl, whisk the melted butter, garlic, lemon juice, chipotle sauce, and cilantro together until well blended; keep warm.

Prepare a medium-hot fire with a kiss of smoke (see page 17) in your grill. We recommend using alder, apple, hickory, oak, pecan, or mesquite wood for smoking.

Place the oysters in the half shell on the grill grates. Dab each with a little Chipotle-Garlic-Cilantro Butter or leave plain to enjoy with Smoky Cocktail Sauce after grilling. When you see the first wisp of smoke, close the lid. Grill for 2 to 3 minutes without peeping, or until the oysters start to frill at the edges and the butter has slightly browned around the oyster. Using grill mitts, place the oysters on platters and serve with your desired sauce.

→ GRILLED OYSTERS WITH SAUCE ON THE SIDE ←

Grilled, broiled, baked, or raw, oysters double the pleasure when they're accompanied with a flavorful sauce.

- Hog Island Oyster Company on Tomales Bay in California serves its grilled Hog Island Sweetwaters with chili butter.
- Eventide Oyster Company in Portland, Maine, serves its Winter Points with Korean-style barbecue sauce, potent with fermented black bean purée and fresh ginger.
- B&G Oysters in Boston, Massachusetts, serves its Wellfleets with a roasted red pepper butter.
- L&E Oyster Bar in Los Angeles, California, serves its Kumamotos with stone crab butter.
- Central Oyster Bar in New York City pairs its Bluepoints with anchovy butter; its grilled farm-style Target Rock oysters feature a confetti butter of colored vegetables and garlic.
- Pearl Dive Oyster Palace in Washington, D.C., loads its Old Black Salts and other Eastern varieties with red chile butter and gremolata.
- Casamento's in New Orleans gives its char-grilled oysters a Parmesan crust after grilling.
- At GT Fish & Oyster in Chicago, Illinois, East and West Coast oysters are paired with Midwestern-grown horseradish.
- The Walrus and the Carpenter in Seattle, Washington, amps up the flavor with garlicky snail butter.

CAJUN GRILLED GULF SHRIMP
with HORSERADISH CREAM SAUCE

Classic shrimp cocktail gets a grilled and chilled makeover in this recipe. Dusted with a spicy Cajun rub and revved up even more with a dollop of Horseradish Cream Sauce—it's new again.

Serves 8

HORSERADISH CREAM SAUCE

$^1/_2$ cup (120 ml) heavy whipping cream

$^1/_2$ cup (115 g) sour cream

1 tablespoon prepared horseradish, or more to taste

CAJUN GRILLED GULF SHRIMP

1 pound (454 g) jumbo shrimp, peeled and deveined

$1^1/_2$ tablespoons Cajun-style spice mixture or Blackening Spice Rub (page 32)

2 cups (85 g) shredded lettuce

1 tomato, seeded and chopped

1 lemon

Olive oil

Kosher salt and freshly ground black pepper

For the Horseradish Cream Sauce, stir together the cream and sour cream in a small bowl until well blended. Cover and leave at room temperature for several hours or overnight (this helps it to thicken). When ready to serve, stir in the horseradish.

Place the shrimp in a plastic bag and add the Cajun spice mixture. Shake to coat the shrimp. Oil the interior and exterior of a grill wok and set on a baking sheet. Pour the shrimp into the wok.

Prepare a hot fire in your grill.

Place the wok filled with shrimp directly over the fire. Stir-grill, tossing with wooden paddles every 2 minutes or so, for 15 minutes, or until the shrimp are pink and opaque.

To serve, arrange the shredded lettuce and chopped tomato on a platter. Squeeze the lemon over the lettuce and then drizzle lightly with olive oil. Set a bowl of the Horseradish Cream Sauce in the center of the platter and surround it with the grilled shrimp. Serve hot, at room temperature, or cold.

PECAN-SMOKED GOAT CHEESE–STUFFED PEPPADEWS

Pecan trees, a botanical cousin to hickory, are native to the southern and south central United States, ranging from Georgia and Alabama west to Missouri, Kansas, and Oklahoma. Native pecan nuts are smaller than commercial varieties; pecan wood is great for wood grilling as well as smoking, with a slightly sweeter smoke than hickory. Peppadews are small, red piquanté peppers that are great for stuffing. You can often find them in bulk in the olive bar section of better grocery stores, but you can also find them in glass jars. The trick is to select well-formed, sweet peppers that are intact. Filled with a little local goat cheese and smoked over pecan wood, these sophisticated poppers combine sweet, pungent, smoky, creamy, and salty flavors—perfect for cocktail hour. Serve these, garnished with fresh rosemary branches, on a white platter for a colorful presentation. Create an edible tic-tac-toe arrangement if you like. A single stuffed Peppadew on a small white appetizer plate would also make an elegant amuse-bouche. Don't plan on leftovers.

Serves 4 to 6

8 ounces (227 g) fresh goat cheese, at room temperature

16 brined red or golden Peppadews

Olive oil

Kosher salt and freshly ground black pepper

Fresh rosemary branches, for garnish

Prepare a fire in your smoker using pecan wood (see page 18).

Using a spoon or a small spatula, stuff about a teaspoon of goat cheese into each Peppadew. Brush with olive oil and season with salt and pepper. Place the peppers, stuffed-side up, in small aluminum pans that will fit on your smoker.

Place the pans on the smoker, cover, and smoke for 45 minutes, or until the peppers have a burnished appearance and a smoky aroma. Serve the Peppadews on a white platter and garnish with rosemary branches.

GRILLED CHICKEN SKEWERS *with* STRAWBERRY RHUBARB BBQ SAUCE

After a trip to the farmers' market, add pops of color and flavor when you serve your grilled chicken skewers. A few scattered blackberries, thinly sliced radishes, green onions, and strawberries create a lively platform for these goodies brushed with Strawberry Rhubarb BBQ Sauce. And here's a new method for chicken skewers—grill the chicken first, then skewer them for serving. Much faster! Much easier, too, is using a prepared, already-delicious barbecue sauce and doctoring it up with fresh ingredients. Sweet Baby Ray's barbecue sauce won the 1985 Mike Royko Rib-Off in Chicago and never looked back. So make a delicious store-bought barbecue sauce your own by adding a finely chopped jalapeño. Sweeten it up with a spoonful of honey or maple syrup. Make it a bit more acidic or tart by adding freshly squeezed lemon juice or white vinegar.

Serves 6

STRAWBERRY RHUBARB BBQ SAUCE

2 pounds (1 kg) fresh strawberries, hulled

8 ounces (227 g) fresh rhubarb stalks, cut into 2-inch (5 cm) pieces

1 (18-ounce/510 g) bottle sweet tomato-based barbecue sauce, such as Sweet Baby Ray's

1/4 cup (60 ml) bourbon

GRILLED CHICKEN SKEWERS

2 boneless, skinless chicken breasts, trimmed and each cut vertically into 6 long pieces

Olive oil

Kosher salt and freshly ground black pepper

12 wooden skewers

For the sauce, preheat the oven to 425°F (218°C). Line a large baking sheet with parchment paper. Arrange the strawberries and rhubarb on the prepared baking sheet. Roast for 15 minutes, or until the strawberries start to shrivel and the rhubarb has softened. Transfer the strawberries and rhubarb to a food processor or high-speed blender, along with any juices. Add the barbecue sauce and bourbon and process until smooth. Use right away or cover and store in the refrigerator for up to 1 week (makes about 2½ cups/600 ml).

In a large, resealable plastic bag, combine the chicken pieces with 1 cup (240 ml) of the barbecue sauce (reserve the remaining sauce). Seal the bag and toss to coat the chicken. Let marinate for at least 1 hour or overnight in the refrigerator.

Prepare a medium-hot fire in your grill.

Remove the chicken pieces from the marinade, discard the marinade, and pat dry with paper towels. Brush with olive oil and season with salt and pepper. Place the pieces perpendicular to the grill grates so

1 cup (95 g) blackberries

1 cup (95 g) hulled strawberries, halved lengthwise

6 green onions, chopped (white and green parts)

3 radishes, trimmed and sliced paper-thin

they don't fall through. Grill for 2 minutes per side, turning once, or until an instant-read thermometer inserted in the center of a chicken strip registers 160°F (71°C). Carefully thread each grilled chicken strip onto a skewer.

To serve, arrange the blackberries, strawberries, green onions, and radish slices in a freeform design on each plate. Drizzle with a little barbecue sauce. Arrange the chicken skewers on top and drizzle with more barbecue sauce. Serve the remaining sauce on the side.

GRILLED RAINBOW CARROT FRIES
with ROASTED PEPPER KETCHUP

This colorful and flavorful take on fries with ketchup has multigenerational appeal. The "ketchup" gets great taste from the vegetables and protein from quinoa, a high-altitude plant now grown in places like White Mountain Farm in the Colorado Rockies. Rainbow carrots—in pale yellow, maroon, orange, purple, and cream—are grown on farms in cooler regions; grab a bunch at RI Organic Farm Market in Rhode Island, for example. The ketchup is also delicious on sandwiches or with other grilled vegetables.

Serves a crowd

ROASTED PEPPER KETCHUP

¹/₂ cup (113 g) white quinoa

1 cup (240 ml) water

¹/₂ cup (113 g) crushed tomatoes

2 tablespoons tomato-based barbecue sauce

2 garlic cloves, minced

3 whole grilled piquillo peppers or roasted red peppers from a jar

1 teaspoon dried basil

1 teaspoon freshly squeezed lemon juice

1 teaspoon honey

¹/₂ cup (120 ml) olive oil

Kosher salt

GRILLED RAINBOW CARROT FRIES

2 pounds (1 kg) rainbow carrots, preferably organic, rinsed and ends trimmed

Olive oil

Kosher salt

1 lemon

For the ketchup, combine the quinoa and water in a medium saucepan and bring to a boil over medium-high heat. Reduce the heat to a simmer, cover, and let cook for 15 minutes, or until the quinoa is soft. Drain off any remaining water and place the quinoa in a blender or food processor. Add the tomatoes, barbecue sauce, garlic, peppers, basil, lemon juice, and honey and purée for several seconds. With the machine running, add the olive oil in a thin stream until the ketchup thickens. Season with salt. You should end up with 2½ cups (60 ml). Use right away or store, covered, in the refrigerator for up to 1 week.

Prepare a medium-hot fire in your grill.

Cut the carrots into thin, 6-inch- (15 cm-) long pieces, like French fries. Arrange on a large baking sheet, toss with olive oil, and season with salt.

Place the carrots on a perforated grill rack or a cast-iron griddle and grill for 15 to 20 minutes, turning often, until the carrots have softened and scorched. The carrots will curl a bit. Transfer the carrots back to the baking sheet and squeeze a little lemon juice over them.

Serve in paper cones with a dollop of "ketchup" in the bottom. Or ring the carrots around the inside of a glass jelly jar and dollop the ketchup in the bottom of the jar.

FROM GARDEN TO GRILL TO GLASS:
→ BBQ COCKTAILS ←

When the sizzle of the grill meets the whiskey sour and other classic libations, good things happen. Aromatizing cocktails with sizzle and smoke can be done in several ways: with smoke-infused liquors, blasting bourbon with a smoking gun (sort of a pistol that shoots aromatic smoke into liquids), using smoked salts or smoky bitters and already-smoked ingredients like chipotles or bacon, or grilling and smoking your own ingredients (herbs, persimmon, butternut squash, lemons, rhubarb) to create a signature drink.

Grilled Lemon Whiskey Sour. Grill the cut sides of lemon halves. The grill marks give a smoky flavor to the fruit and caramelize the juices into something really wonderful. For each cocktail, mix the juice of a grilled lemon half with 2 ounces (60 ml) whiskey or small-batch bourbon and 1 ounce (30 ml) simple syrup and pour over a glass of ice. You can also get a smoky flavor by skipping the simple syrup and lemon and mixing your favorite bourbon with Bittermilk No. 3 Smoked Honey Whiskey Sour; the honey is smoked over barrel staves. Makes 1 cocktail.

Grilled Persimmon and Smoked Thyme Cocktail. Cut a ripe Fuyu persimmon in half and grill the cut sides until you have good grill marks. Purée the persimmon pulp and discard the skin. Mix 2 ounces (60 ml) grilled persimmon purée with 2 ounces (60 ml) simple syrup, 1 ounce (45 ml) freshly squeezed lemon juice, 4 ounces (120 ml) whiskey, and a dash or two of bitters. Shake with ice and then strain the drink into 2 glasses. Hold a branch of fresh thyme over each glass (with most of the leaves above the liquid) and use a long grill match to light and smolder the fresh thyme for a few seconds before blowing it out. The smoldering thyme aromatizes the drink, and the tiny singed thyme leaves that fall into the drink give it a slightly smoky flavor. Adapted from a recipe by Ashley Rose Conway at CraftandCocktails.co [not com]. Makes 2 cocktails.

Smoked Bloody Mary with Bacon. The classic Bloody Mary is a fabulous blank canvas for smoky flavors. Use a smoke- or bacon-infused vodka or naturally smoky mezcal as the alcohol. Smoke tomatoes on your grill for 1 hour and juice them (also double-smoke your bacon) as Mary Cressler does at Vindulge.com. For 4 drinks, she smokes 4 to 5 Roma tomatoes, removes the skins, and then purées them in a blender. Then, to the blender, she adds 3 cups (720 ml) more tomato juice, 1 tablespoon Worcestershire, 2 teaspoons prepared horseradish, a little hot sauce, the juice of a lemon, and salt and pepper. For each drink, she figures 1 to 2 ounces (30 to 60 ml) of vodka, and then tops it off with the smoky tomato mix. She even makes smoked ice cubes by placing a pan of water on the smoker, smoking the water for an hour, and then using the smoked water to make ice cubes.

Grilled Fruit Sangria. Simply grill slices of orange and pineapple and blister whole clusters of grapes (or use a perforated grill pan to contain them). Chop the fruit into smaller pieces and cut each grape in half; the fruit goes into a large pitcher. Pour in 1½ liters of a chilled, fruity red wine, ½ cup (120 ml) Calvados, ½ cup (120 ml) brandy, and maybe some simple syrup to taste. A good stir, and the sangria is ready to serve over a glass of ice. Adapted from a recipe by Mike Vrobel of Dad-CooksDinner.com. Makes a pitcher of sangria.

CHAPTER 2

Sandwiches, Subs, Sliders, Burgers, Tacos & 'Dogs

THE QUINTESSENTIAL AMERICAN SANDWICH HAS GOT TO BE the PB&J, doesn't it? Or would it be a BLT? Whatever kind of sandwich you decide to make, make it good. We offer an artisan Smoky Grilled-Grilled Cheese (page 52) with crunchy, toasty goodness and a twist on the kind of smoked cheeses and extras you can pile on it, and Smoked Fish Tacos (page 70), rather than the typical "grilled," that are as good or better than any fish tacos you've had in a restaurant.

Panini has become Americanized, too. These elegant, thin, and crisp pressed sandwiches do well on the grill when weighted down with a foil-covered brick. Our Smoked Corned Beef Reuben Panini (page 54) is a nod to all the wonderful delicatessen Reubens—much thinner but still delicious.

Another plus to making premium handhelds is in the sauce, spread, dressing, and bun. The queen of sandwich spreads has long been mayonnaise—Duke's if you're south of the Mason-Dixon line, Hellman's if you're north. But other choices now include a drizzle of vinaigrette, a slather of artisan mustard, a smear of great chipotle BBQ sauce, or a spread of delicious compound butter. Artisan bakery bread and buns can take a burger from good to great, plus we toast all of our buns on the grill with a slather of olive oil or butter blended with mustard.

For a large gathering, grilling up some gourmet burgers can be as easy as setting out a fantastic spread of fillings, toppings, and condiments. Start with a combination of ground meat lightly formed into patties (see Daily Grind, page 67); an assortment of sliced cheeses; pickle and olive relishes; garnishes like sliced tomatoes, cucumbers, onions, lettuces, mushrooms, and even summer squash; spreads like assorted mustards, aioli, mayonnaise, BBQ sauce like our Cherry Chipotle Barbecue Sauce (page 128), flavored butters from our Butter-Up Chart (see page 161); and a basket of wonderful artisan bakery breads and buns.

Want to make a great sandwich better? Embellish should be your byword.

★ ★ ★

Smoky Grilled-Grilled Cheese

Smoked Corned Beef Reuben Panini

Grilled Farmers' Market Sandwich

Great Big Grilled Pizza Sandwich

Grilled Shrimp Po' Boy

Grilled Meatball Hoagies

BBQ Sliders

Grilled Lamb Patty Sliders

Bison Burger Sliders

Grilled Chicken Caesar on Ciabatta

Veggie Sliders with Herbed Cream Cheese

Grilled Turkey and Arugula Burgers

Smoky Brisket Burgers

Smoked Fish Tacos with Napa Cabbage Slaw

Smoked Garlic and Fresh Lime Ajo

Smoked Cashew Crema

Grilled Yellow Squash, Corn, and Pepper Tacos

Grilled Zucchini and Fresh Cucumber Roll-Ups

Cross-Hatched Hot Dogs on a Stick

Grilled Brats with Horseradish Butter

Grilled Artisan Sausages

★ ★ ★

SMOKY GRILLED-GRILLED CHEESE

We take a simple grilled cheese sandwich to smoky, fantastic heights with this recipe. It's garden fresh with slices of tomato, peppers, and onions that are the perfect acidic foil to the rich, creamy cheese. If it is fall or winter and the tomatoes are not so great, omit them and add slices of pickled pepperoncini sprinkled over the cheese along with the red onion slices. Or for a sublime meat treat, add smoked brisket to this classic and be prepared to swoon. You can find smoked cheeses at a gourmet cheese store or grocer who offers a well-stocked cheese counter. Here are a couple of artisan smoked cheeses to look for: Up in Smoke from Rivers Edge Chèvre in Oregon is smoked with alder and hickory (remove the smoky leaf wrapping first), and Oregon Blue by Rogue Creamery is cold-smoked with Oregon hazelnut shells. Trade out the cheeses for whatever suits your fancy. It's your sandwich! For a summer lunch or supper, serve this with Char-Grilled Tomato and Red Bell Pepper Soup with a bacon, feta, and chive Banner (page 105)!

Serves 4

8 slices sourdough bread

¼ cup (56 g) unsalted butter, at room temperature

4 slices smoked Cheddar cheese

4 to 8 slices tomato

4 slices smoked Gouda cheese

2 banana peppers or jalapeños, seeded and sliced

8 thin slices red onion

4 to 8 slices smoked Gruyère cheese

Prepare a medium-hot fire in your grill.

Lightly butter one side of each piece of bread. Place 4 slices of the bread, butter-side down, on a baking sheet. Assemble the sandwiches, beginning with a Cheddar cheese slice to cover each, followed by 1 or 2 slices of tomato, a slice of Gouda, a quarter of the sliced peppers, 2 slices of red onion, and ending with 1 or 2 slices of Gruyère. Set the other piece of bread on top, butter-side up. Use the baking sheet to carry the sandwiches to the grill. Place the sandwiches directly on the grill grates and grill the sandwiches for about 4 or 5 minutes on each side, or longer, depending on how browned you like your sandwich.

SMOKED CORNED BEEF REUBEN PANINI

Whether originating in a New York deli (to serve an actress in a Charlie Chaplin movie) or in Omaha, Nebraska (to serve poker buddies), the Reuben was too good to stay in one place. Now it has moved to the grill. To grill a Reuben, simply cover bricks with heavy-duty foil for weights, use a heavy cast-iron skillet as a weight, or simply press down hard on the panini with heavy-duty grill spatulas. It is best not to load up a panini with too much filling or spreads, as the ingredients will ooze out when pressed. The crispy bread is what you are going for in this recipe. Not a corned beef fan? Substitute smoked brisket!

Serves 4

8 slices rye or pumpernickel
  bakery bread
Olive oil, for brushing
German mustard (optional)
8 slices Swiss cheese
8 thin slices corned beef
1 cup (160 g) sauerkraut

Take 4 slices of the bread, brush one side of each with olive oil, and place them, oiled-side down, on a baking sheet. Lightly spread the top sides of the bread with the mustard, if using, then top each with 1 slice of cheese, 2 slices of corned beef, ¼ cup (40 g) sauerkraut, and another slice of cheese. Top with the remaining slice of bread, and brush the top with olive oil.

Prepare a medium-hot fire in your grill. Have ready 4 foil-wrapped bricks to press down the sandwiches.

Place each sandwich on the grill rack and press down with a foil-wrapped brick. Grill for 3 to 4 minutes on each side, or until they have good grill marks and the cheese has melted.

⟶ CLUB SANDWICHES ⟵

The first club sandwich recipe dates back to 1903, from the *Good Housekeeping Everyday Cook Book*, as a simple toasted sandwich layered with a crisp piece of bacon, sliced turkey or chicken, a tomato slice, a tender piece of lettuce, and a slather of mayonnaise. Before this, the sandwich had been served at country clubs and linked originally to the Saratoga Club in upstate New York. The St. Louis World's Fair offered the club with potato chips at as many as four restaurants, which helped to popularize the sandwich. We like how *James Beard's American Cookery* book (1972) sums it up: ". . . it is one of the great sandwiches of all time and has swept its way around the world after an American beginning. Nowadays the sandwich is bastardized because it is usually made as a three-decker, which is not authentic (whoever started that horror should be forced to eat three-deckers three times a day the rest of his life), and nowadays practically everyone uses turkey and there's a vast difference between turkey and chicken where sandwiches are concerned."

So, Mr. Beard, here is our nod—with a bit of modernizing.

★ ★ ★

Grilled Chicken Club Sandwich to Serve One

2 pieces good-quality bread from a bakery,
buttered and grilled for about 1 minute on each side for good grill marks

A slathering of Smoky Garlic Aioli (page 155) on one side of each piece of grilled bread

Then layer the following ingredients on the bread:

1 thin chicken breast brushed with olive oil,
grilled over high heat for about 2 minutes on each side

2 pieces crisp cooked bacon

2 tablespoons Tomato-Avocado Relish (page 37)

1 lovely piece butter lettuce

Top with the other piece of grilled bread and slice on the diagonal.
Insert a toothpick to hold the sandwich together for a nostalgic presentation.

GRILLED FARMERS' MARKET SANDWICH

This easy sandwich makes for a great casual meal for friends and family both. It's so easy to put together, you can have your kids assemble the sandwich, if you wish. Feel free to substitute herbed cream cheese for goat cheese, or slather more pesto and goat cheese on the tops and bottoms of the sandwiches if you like. You may assemble the sandwich, wrap it in aluminum foil, and store it in the refrigerator in the morning, to grill for dinner that night. If you are a meat lover, add some very thin slices of your favorite salami.

Serves 4 to 6

1 large round or oblong loaf fresh Italian bread

Olive oil, for brushing

8 ounces (227 g) soft goat cheese, or more to taste

¼ cup (56 g) prepared pesto, or more to taste

6 large tomatoes, thinly sliced

Kosher salt and freshly ground black pepper

1 cucumber, thinly sliced

1 cup (142 g) pitted and sliced olives, such as Kalamata

4 large jarred roasted red pepper halves

½ cup (71 g) chopped marinated artichoke hearts

Cut the Italian bread in half lengthwise (so you have a top and a bottom) and turn the cut sides up. With your fingers or a fork, hollow out about one-third of the top half of the bread and set aside (discard or reserve the scooped-out insides for another use, like the bread-crumbs on page 147). Brush the bottom half with olive oil, then spread it with the goat cheese, followed by the pesto. Next, layer the slices of tomato to cover, season with salt and pepper, and top with a layer of the cucumber slices. Now add the olives, roasted red peppers, and artichoke hearts. Brush the hollowed top half of the bread with olive oil and place on top of the sandwich fillings. Wrap well in heavy-duty aluminum foil.

Prepare a medium fire in your grill.

Grill the sandwich in the foil, covered, turning once, until heated through, 20 to 25 minutes. Remove the foil and cut with a serrated knife into 4 to 6 slices and serve warm or at room temperature.

GREAT BIG GRILLED PIZZA SANDWICH

The same ingredients that go into a supreme pizza can taste wonderful in a grilled sandwich. Now that you can buy already-cooked sausage crumbles, it makes preparation that much easier. If you can't find the precooked sausage, substitute Canadian bacon or ham, or precook about 5 to 6 ounces of sausage. If you want to be thrifty, you can save the scooped-out insides of the bread, let them dry for a day or two, and grate them for home-made breadcrumbs. You can also prepare this sandwich earlier in the day, wrap it in foil, and refrigerate it, so all you have left to do later is grill it.

Serves 4 to 6

1 large loaf fresh Italian or French bread

²/₃ cup (153 g) pizza sauce of your choice

¹/₂ cup (50 g) pepperoni slices

¹/₂ cup (57 g) cooked crumbled Italian sausage or regular pork or turkey sausage

¹/₂ cup (75 g) finely chopped red onion

¹/₂ cup (88 g) finely chopped green bell pepper

¹/₂ cup (75 g) pitted and sliced olives, such as Kalamata

¹/₂ cup (75 g) muffaletta mix from the grocery store olive bar or jarred Italian olive salad

8 slices mozzarella or provolone cheese, or a combination

Olive oil, for brushing

Cut the Italian bread in half lengthwise (so you have a top and a bottom) and turn the cut sides up. With your fingers or a fork, hollow out about one-third of the top half of the bread and set aside (discard or reserve the scooped-out insides for another use, like the breadcrumbs on page 147). Brush the bottom half with olive oil, then spread the bottom half with the pizza sauce. Layer on the pepperoni, sausage, onion, bell pepper, olives, muffaletta mix, and slices of cheese. Brush the hollowed top half of the bread with olive oil and place on top of the sandwich fillings. Wrap well in heavy-duty aluminum foil.

Prepare a medium fire in your grill.

Grill the loaf in the foil, covered, turning once, until heated through, 20 to 25 minutes. Remove the foil and cut with a serrated knife into 4 to 6 slices and serve hot.

GRILLED SHRIMP PO' BOY

Louisiana claims the po' boy sandwich and kicks up the heat with a shake of its hot sauce. Traditionally dressed with a slather of mayonnaise, chopped romaine lettuce, sliced tomatoes and pickles, our version adds a Smoky Remoulade Sauce made with smoked paprika. The sauce makes plenty and keeps in the refrigerator for several days. Use it on deli sandwiches, burgers, or grilled vegetables, or dollop it in the middle of a platter of tomatoes.

Serves 4

SMOKY REMOULADE SAUCE

1¼ cups (284 g) mayonnaise

¼ cup (57 g) Creole mustard

1 garlic clove, minced

1 tablespoon smoked paprika

2 teaspoons Cajun seasoning or Blackening Spice Rub (page 32)

2 teaspoons prepared horseradish

2 teaspoons freshly squeezed lemon juice

½ teaspoon hot sauce

GRILLED SHRIMP

1 pound (454 g) medium to large shrimp, peeled and deveined

Olive oil

Kosher salt and freshly ground black pepper

4 mini baguettes or hoagie buns

1 tomato, thinly sliced

1 red onion, thinly sliced

1 cup (42 g) shredded greens, such as oak leaf, red leaf, or Boston lettuce

Prepare a hot fire in your grill and oil both sides of a grill basket or wok.

For the Smoky Remoulade Sauce, combine all the ingredients in a bowl and stir to blend. The sauce will keep, covered, in the refrigerator for several days.

In a bowl, combine the shrimp with a drizzle of olive oil and season with salt and pepper. Pour the shrimp into the grill basket or wok and set directly over the hot fire. Toss with long-handled tongs or wooden spoons until the shrimp are almost done, about 4 to 5 minutes.

Slice the buns open, not quite cutting all the way through so that tops and bottoms are connected. Lightly brush the cut side of the buns with olive oil. Grill the buns, cut-side down, for about 30 seconds and set aside.

Pour the grilled shrimp into a clean bowl and spoon the desired amount of Smoky Remoulade Sauce over the shrimp, tossing to coat.

Place sliced tomatoes on one side of the buns and sliced onions on the other side. Spoon the dressed shrimp down the middle of each sandwich and top with shredded lettuce.

GRILLED MEATBALL HOAGIES

When grilling any kind of meatballs, we recommend using a meatball grilling basket. It holds twelve large meatballs and is easy to turn to grill the other side of the meatballs. This recipe makes about sixteen meatballs, so just place the extras on the grill grates and turn them individually. The flavor from this simple recipe comes from good-quality ground meat and the char from the grill. They are so good that you can skip making the sandwich and just eat the meatballs!

Serves 6

- 1 pound (454 g) ground pork
- 1 pound (454 g) ground beef, venison, bison, or turkey
- ³/₄ cup (75 g) grated Parmesan cheese
- 1¹/₂ teaspoons kosher salt
- 1¹/₂ cups (340 g) of your favorite marinara sauce
- 4 bakery-fresh hoagie buns
- Olive oil, for brushing
- 1 cup (113 g) freshly grated Parmesan, Romano, or mozzarella cheese, for garnish

Prepare a hot fire in your grill.

For the meatballs, combine the ground meats, Parmesan cheese, and salt with a light touch and form into meatballs. You should have about 16 golf ball–sized meatballs.

Heat the marinara sauce, cover, and keep warm.

Slice the buns open, not quite cutting all the way through so that tops and bottoms are connected. Lightly brush the cut side of the buns with olive oil and grill them, cut-side down, for about 30 to 45 seconds.

If you have a meatball basket, fill it with the meatballs. Grill the meatballs for about 4 to 5 minutes per side, or until charred, turning the basket once. At the same time, grill any additional meatballs that don't fit in the basket directly on the grates, turning them once for good grill marks, 4 to 5 minutes per side.

Set 2 or 3 meatballs onto each open hoagie and spoon ¼ cup (58 g) warm marinara sauce over the meatballs. Garnish with freshly grated cheese.

BBQ Sliders

Sliders are typically little ground-beef patties on a small bun. Originally, the larger hamburger, also referred to as a Hamburg steak, gained national recognition in 1904 at the St. Louis World's Fair. After World War I, however, anti-German sentiment made the term unpopular. That's why Hamburg steaks became Salisbury steaks—and the stories go on. White Castle introduced small, 2½-inch (6.3 cm) hamburgers served on small, soft buns and named them sliders. Americans bought them by the bagful and ate them up.

Now sliders appear on happy hour menus as an appetizer, and even as an entrée when served as a trio. Our recipes are for happy hour, which means they have to be easy to hold. If you load the slider with lots of extras like avocado slices, lettuce, tomato, relishes, strips of bacon, slices of mushrooms, slaw, and such, they probably will fall apart. Of course, if you are serving the sliders on plates and sitting around a table, fill them up, but serve them with forks!

GRILLED LAMB PATTY SLIDERS

The award-winning Memphis Blues Barbeque House in Vancouver hosted a media event for us a few years ago. As we mingled and sipped our first cocktail, they served a platter of grilled lamb patty sliders with a small dollop of mint jelly. They were small, simple, and delicious, easy to hold and eat while standing with a drink in the other hand.

Makes 8 sliders

1 pound (454 g) ground lamb
2 garlic cloves, minced
1 teaspoon kosher salt
Freshly ground black pepper
8 small slider buns
Butter, at room temperature
  for spreading
Dijon mustard
Mint jelly

Prepare a hot fire in your grill.

Combine the ground lamb, garlic, and salt, season with pepper, and mix lightly. Divide the mixture into 8 equal portions and form into thin patties. The patties will shrink as they cook, so they need to be bigger than the buns while raw.

Lightly butter the cut sides of the buns and grill, cut-side down, for 30 seconds. Lightly spread Dijon mustard on the grilled sides of the buns and set aside.

Grill the patties for 3 minutes per side for medium-rare. Place a patty on each bottom bun and sprinkle lightly with salt and pepper. Dollop a small spoonful of mint jelly on top of each patty. Top with the remaining bun and serve hot.

BISON BURGER SLIDERS

Lean bison is best cooked medium-rare. If you want a guaranteed juicier slider, add ¹/₄ pound (113 g) ground pork to the ground bison. If you want these to be quarter-pounders, divide the mixture into four equal portions. Buy artisan buns like Kaiser, ciabatta, or hoagie-shaped ones. Then shape the burger to fit your bun. You can add your favorite cheeses and any other condiment fixin's.

Makes 8 sliders

1 pound (454 g) ground bison

1 teaspoon kosher salt

Freshly ground black pepper

8 small buns

Butter, at room temperature
  for spreading

Dijon mustard

Mayonnaise

Dill pickle slices

1 red onion, thinly sliced

Prepare a hot fire in your grill.

Combine the ground bison and salt, season with pepper, and mix lightly. Divide the mixture into 8 equal portions and form into thin patties. The patties will shrink as they cook, so they need to be bigger than the buns while raw.

Lightly butter the cut sides of the buns and grill, cut-side down, for 30 seconds. Lightly spread Dijon mustard and mayonnaise on the grilled sides of the buns and set aside.

Grill the patties for 3 minutes per side for medium-rare. Place a patty on each bottom bun, sprinkle lightly with salt and pepper, and top with a couple of pickle slices and a slice of red onion. Top with the remaining bun and serve hot.

VEGGIE SLIDERS
with HERBED CREAM CHEESE

Here is a nod to anyone who wants to forgo the meat patty. Let this be a guide for you to add other vegetables like grilled slices of eggplant, zucchini, tomato, or onions. Garnish with fresh tender greens, pea shoots, or sprouts, if desired. If you like, substitute Boursin instead of making our cream cheese spread (which is delectable and rather inexpensive in comparison).

Makes 8 sliders

HERBED CREAM CHEESE
1 garlic clove, minced

1 tablespoon chopped fresh parsley

1 (8-ounce/227 g) package cream cheese, at room temperature

4 ounces (113 g) unsalted butter, at room temperature

1/4 teaspoon kosher salt

1/4 teaspoon ground white pepper

SLIDERS
4 red bell peppers

8 small buns

Butter, at room temperature for spreading

1 red onion, thinly sliced

For the Herbed Cream Cheese, in a bowl, combine the garlic, parsley, cream cheese, butter, salt, and pepper, and stir until smooth. This spread will keep in the refrigerator for a week or more.

Prepare a hot fire in your grill.

Grill the peppers, turning every few minutes, until they have good grill marks all over. Remove the peppers from the grill and place them in a paper or plastic bag, close the bag, and let them steam until they're cool enough to handle. Then stem, seed, and cut each pepper into 4 slices. Rub off the charred skin if you like.

Lightly butter the cut sides of the buns and grill, cut-side down, for 30 seconds.

Spread the herbed cream cheese on both cut sides of each bun. Layer 2 pieces of pepper on each bottom bun and top with a slice of red onion and the top of the bun. Serve warm.

—→ Daily Grind ←—

If you want a truly signature grilled burger big on flavor, if you want to
know exactly what went into it, and if you like superior texture, then you might want to
grind your own beef. Stand mixers have a meat-grinding attachment, or you can have a
full-service meat department grind it for you. For thin, flat burgers that you would cook
in a hot skillet, a finer grind (using the ¼-inch/.64 cm grinding plate) results in a better,
darker crust. But over a hot fire, you want the burgers thicker in order to stay juicy and
hold together during grilling, so use the ¾-inch (1.9 cm) grinding plate.

1. Choose the best cuts, such as chuck, which has a nice balance of fat to lean (20–24% fat
is a great ratio for good flavor and moistness). For deeper flavor, you might grind equal
parts brisket and chuck together. Pork shoulder has great flavor and fat content for
grinding into burgers, too.

2. Cut the meat into cubes and chill in the freezer for 30 minutes before grinding. Also
freeze the grinding plate and other cutting parts for 30 minutes before grinding.

3. Quickly assemble the cold grinding attachment.

4. Place the chilled meat in the hopper, turn the mixer on, and push the meat into the
grinder.

5. For tender burgers, lightly mix 1 pound of ground meat and 1 teaspoon kosher salt,
plus any other additions you desire. Lightly form the freshly ground meat into patties.

6. Fire up the grill! (Avoid pressing down on the patties while they are cooking. You don't
want to lose that delicious juice.)

GRILLED CHICKEN CAESAR *on* CIABATTA

Here is one of the most popular salads today—on a bun. Our fresh take in this includes grilled chicken on wonderful artisan ciabatta bread with a zippy Caesar dressing, which is good on all kinds of grilled food. If you have leftover grilled chicken breast, this sandwich becomes even easier. If not, a paillard or boneless skinless chicken breast pounded thin only takes minutes to cook on a hot grill. Use a vegetable peeler to shave shards of Parmesan for the sandwich. Salmon, a hamburger, or sliced steak are good substitutes for chicken, if you like.

Serves 4

CAESAR DRESSING

5 tablespoons (70 g) mayonnaise

1 to 2 teaspoons anchovy paste, to taste

1 garlic clove, minced, or more to taste

1 teaspoon Dijon mustard

1 tablespoon freshly squeezed lemon juice

Kosher salt and freshly ground black pepper

$^1/_3$ cup (38 g) freshly grated Parmesan cheese

SANDWICHES

2 loaves ciabatta or 4 ciabattini (ciabatta rolls), sliced in half lengthwise

Olive oil for brushing

4 boneless skinless chicken breasts, pounded to a $^1/_2$-inch (1.27 cm) thickness, or chicken paillards

Kosher salt and freshly ground black pepper

Small wedge of Parmesan cheese for shaving

2 cups (160 g) torn romaine lettuce leaves

Whisk together all the dressing ingredients in a small bowl and set aside. If you like your Caesar a little zippier, add more anchovy paste and garlic. You should have about $^2/_3$ cup (160 ml), which is more than you will need for the sandwiches. Refrigerate any leftover dressing for a day or two and use it on salads, crudité, or other sandwiches.

Prepare a hot fire in your grill.

Brush the cut sides of the ciabatta with olive oil and place on a baking sheet. Brush the chicken breasts with olive oil on both sides and season with salt and pepper. Place on a plate on the baking sheet to bring out to the grill.

Grill the chicken, turning once, for 5 minutes total. Grill the ciabatta, cut-sides down, until you have good grill marks, 30 to 60 seconds. Place the chicken breasts on the clean baking sheet with the ciabatta and bring indoors.

Slather the grilled sides of the ciabatta with the dressing. Place the chicken breasts on the bottom half of the bread, shave some Parmesan cheese over the chicken, and then top with lettuce and the top half of the bread. If you're using a loaf of ciabatta, you'll have 2 chicken breasts on each loaf, so cut each loaf in half. If you're using ciabattini, you'll use 1 breast for each roll. Serve immediately.

GRILLED TURKEY
and ARUGULA BURGERS

Good-quality ground turkey is readily available from your grocer's meat counter. Since ground turkey is very lean, it is helpful to bind it with an egg to hold the burger together—especially in this recipe, which we load with freshly chopped arugula and feta cheese. The peppery flavor of arugula ramps up the taste of this burger. Other possible leaves include peppery nasturtium, spinach, or kale. Make sure you oil the grill grates so that it is easier to turn the burgers, which have a tendency to stick.

Serves 4

1 pound (454 g) ground turkey

3 ounces (85 g) arugula, chopped

4 ounces (113 g) feta cheese, crumbled

1 large egg, beaten

3 green onions, thinly sliced (white and green parts)

1 garlic clove, minced

½ teaspoon ground cumin

½ teaspoon kosher salt

½ teaspoon freshly ground black pepper

4 bakery hamburger buns

Olive oil, for brushing

Dijon mustard

Sliced tomatoes, for serving

Sliced red onion, for serving

In a bowl, combine the turkey, arugula, feta, egg, green onion, garlic, cumin, salt, and pepper. Using a fork, mix gently just to combine, and then lightly form into 4 burger patties. Refrigerate, covered, for 30 minutes.

Oil the grill grates and then prepare a medium-hot fire in your grill.

Lightly brush the cut sides of the buns with olive oil and grill, cut-side down, for about 45 seconds. Lightly spread Dijon mustard on the grilled sides of the buns and set aside.

Lightly brush the patties with olive oil. Grill the patties for about 4 to 5 minutes on each side, turning once, until a meat thermometer registers 160°F (71°C) for well-done.

Serve the burgers on the buns with slices of tomato and red onion.

SMOKY BRISKET BURGERS

The Char Bar of Westport in Kansas City introduced us to their awesome smoked brisket burger. Similarly, Q39 in Kansas City serves a beef burger topped with tender slices of smoked brisket. We decided to make our own blend of the two by mixing the ground brisket with ground chuck for an over-the-top smoky, meaty Midwestern burger. These are half-pounders, but you can make them smaller if you wish. For serving a crowd, set out an additional assortment of condiments, including several cheeses, mustards, pickles, hot peppers, and other spreads. Enjoy!

Serves 6

1¹/₂ pounds (680 g) ground brisket

1¹/₂ pounds (680 g) ground chuck

¹/₂ cup (113 g) Sweet Baby Ray's Honey Chipotle Barbecue Sauce or other similar sauce, plus more for serving

2 tablespoons Dijon mustard

2 teaspoons smoked paprika

2 teaspoons hickory-smoked salt (homemade or Tone's salt, or any other brand of smoked salt)

6 Kaiser rolls

Olive oil, for brushing

6 slices tomato

6 slices smoked Gouda cheese

6 slices red onion

6 butter lettuce leaves

12 slices crisply cooked bacon

Prepare a hot fire in your grill.

For the burgers, lightly combine the ground meats, barbecue sauce, mustard, paprika, and salt. Lightly shape into 6 large patties, about 1 inch (2.5 cm) thick (see Daily Grind, page 67).

Lightly brush the cut sides of the buns with olive oil. Grill the buns, cut-side down, for about 30 seconds and set aside.

Grill the burgers for 4 to 5 minutes per side for medium, or to your desired doneness. Place the burgers on a platter alongside the toasted buns. Arrange the tomato, cheese, onion, lettuce, and bacon on another plate and let everyone dress up their own burgers. Pass the extra barbecue sauce.

When Smoke Gets In Your Tacos

Tacos might have originated with Mexican silver miners in the eight-eenth century, says culinary historian Jeffrey M. Pilcher, professor of history at the University of Minnesota. These handheld sandwiches entered the Los Angeles food scene right after World War II. Mexican immigrants had to adapt their recipes that originally used cheaper cuts of meat, Mexican cheeses, and chiles to what was available and cheap in America at that time—ground beef, processed Cheddar cheese, and iceberg lettuce.

Now, we've come full circle. We want tacos with real flavor, fresh ingredients, and a hint of smokiness from the grill. Drizzle your grilled taco fillings—fish, skirt steak, chicken, or vegetables—with Smoked Garlic and Fresh Lime Ajo (page 71) or dollop Smoked Cashew Crema (page 72) on top instead of sour cream. Mmmmmmm.

SMOKED FISH TACOS
with NAPA CABBAGE SLAW

So many people love fish tacos. They are quick, easy, and perfect for weeknights, serving a family in style, and they're tasty enough for company, too. With this recipe you get three versatile components that can mix and match with lots of other recipes. The Lemon Pepper BBQ Rub is bright and flavorful, and you can use it on other kinds of grilled fish, chicken, pork chops, or tenderloin. The Napa Cabbage Slaw would be a tangy slaw for a pulled pork sandwich and works well as a stand-alone side dish. For shellfish tacos, try this recipe with either shrimp or scallops. We suggest using oak or apple wood for smoking. Serve with a crisp beer, such as a lager, or a nice, crisp pinot grigio.

Makes 8 tacos

**LEMON PEPPER
BBQ RUB**

2 tablespoons lemon pepper
1¹/₂ tablespoons ground cumin
1¹/₂ tablespoons ground coriander
1 tablespoon ground chipotle pepper
1 tablespoon packed dark brown sugar

For the Lemon Pepper BBQ Rub, combine all the ingredients in a glass jar. Close the lid and shake to blend. Measure out 4 tablespoons (60 ml) and reserve the rest in the pantry for a couple of months.

For the Napa Cabbage Slaw, combine the cabbage, greens, and green onions in a large bowl. In a small bowl, combine the vinegar, sour cream, lemon juice, and salt to make a dressing. Set aside.

NAPA CABBAGE SLAW

2 cups (84 g) finely chopped
  napa cabbage

1 cup (42 g) assorted baby
  greens, such as spinach, oak
  leaf, or Boston lettuce

8 green onions, chopped
  (white and green parts)

¼ cup (60 ml) tarragon vinegar
  or rice wine vinegar

¼ cup (56 g) sour cream

½ cup (120 ml) freshly squeezed
  lemon juice

½ teaspoon kosher salt

FISH TACOS

1½ pounds (680 g) halibut
  or other mild white fish fillets

8 flour tortillas

8 lemon wedges, for serving

1½ cups (340 g) salsa of
  your choice

Coat the fish fillets with the rub and set them in a disposable aluminum pan.

Prepare a hot fire in your grill or smoker with a kiss of smoke (see page 17); we like oak or apple wood here.

When you see the first wisp of smoke, set the pan of fish over the hot fire. Close the grill lid and grill/smoke for 5 minutes. Turn the fish fillets over and grill/smoke with the lid down for another 3 to 4 minutes, or until the fish begins to flake easily with a fork and is done.

Right before assembling the tacos, pour the dressing over the cabbage mixture and toss to blend. To assemble the tacos, place 3 ounces of grilled fish on each tortilla. Top with about ⅓ cup of the cabbage slaw and roll up. Serve with lemon wedges and small ramekins of salsa.

SMOKED GARLIC *and* FRESH LIME AJO

This aromatic, pungent drizzle goes well with grilled vegetables, fish, or chicken as a finishing sauce.

Makes 1 cup (240 ml)

2 heads smoke-roasted garlic
  (see page 167)

1 cup (240 ml) olive oil

Juice of 1 lime

Kosher salt and freshly
  ground black pepper

Peel and finely chop the garlic and place it in a medium bowl. Stir in the olive oil and lime juice and season with salt and pepper. Serve right away or cover and refrigerate for up to 3 days.

SMOKED CASHEW CREMA

When we were at Empellón Taqueria in New York City's West Village, we savored smoked cashew crema for the first time. This plant-based sour "cream" dolloped on grilled tacos hit the spot. So, we went home and recreated it. Now, we don't advise firing up the smoker just for cashews. Smoke a few other things at the same time, like whole heads of garlic, cherry tomatoes, peppers, or fresh apple halves; pecan or hickory wood is a good choice. Use this topping as you would sour cream or Mexican crema. It's mighty good with grilled fingerling potatoes. Start the cashews the day before you want to use them.

Makes 1½ cups (340 g)

1 cup (125 g) whole raw cashews
1 cup (240 ml) water
Juice of half a lemon
½ teaspoon kosher salt

Prepare a medium-hot indirect fire in your grill or smoker with a kiss of smoke (see page 17), using pecan or hickory wood.

Place the cashews in a disposable aluminum pan and place on the indirect side of your grill or smoker. Close the lid and smoke for 1 hour, or until the cashews are aromatic with smoke and bronzed in color.

Transfer the smoked cashews to a bowl and add the water. Cover and let sit at room temperature for 24 hours.

Transfer the cashews and water to a food processor or high-speed blender and blend until creamy. Add the lemon juice and salt. Serve right away or cover and chill for up to 1 week in the refrigerator.

GRILLED YELLOW SQUASH, CORN, *and* PEPPER TACOS

Instead of making succotash or ratatouille or any of those traditional recipes that celebrate the summer vegetable harvest, why not grill, and turn those same flavors into tacos? Combine the grilled veggies in a skillet with Smoked Cashew Crema or Smoked Garlic and Fresh Lime Ajo (page 71) for an out-of-this-world taco filling.

Serves 4

12 shishito peppers, or 8 banana peppers

2 yellow summer squash, cut into long, 1-inch- (2.5 cm-) thick slices

1 large red onion, cut into thick slices

1 ear sweet corn, shucked and silk removed

Olive oil, for brushing

Kosher salt and freshly ground black pepper

1 cup (227 g) Smoked Cashew Crema (page 72) or sour cream, plus more for garnish, or 1 recipe Smoked Garlic and Fresh Lime Ajo (page 71)

8 flour or corn tortillas

Chopped fresh tomato, for serving

Chopped fresh cilantro, for serving

Prepare a medium-hot fire in your grill.

Place the peppers, summer squash, onion, and ear of corn on a large baking sheet, brush with olive oil, and season with salt and pepper.

Grill the whole peppers, for 2 to 4 minutes, turning as they blister and puff up. Grill the summer squash slices for 4 minutes, turning once, or until they have good grill marks. Grill the onion slices for 5 to 8 minutes, turning once, or until they have good grill marks. Grill the corn for 2 to 4 minutes, turning often, until the kernels scorch. Transfer each item back to the baking sheet once cooked.

Chop the peppers (discarding the stems), summer squash, and onion and place in a grill skillet. Slice the kernels from the corn and add to the skillet. Add the Smoked Cashew Crema or Smoked Garlic and Fresh Lime Ajo. Place the skillet over direct heat and cook, stirring, until the taco filling is heated through, about 4 minutes.

To serve, put a spoonful of taco filling in the center of each tortilla, dollop with more crema or ajo, sprinkle with chopped tomato and cilantro, and wrap up.

GRILLED ZUCCHINI *and* FRESH CUCUMBER ROLL-UPS

No one will miss the bread with this recipe. The grilled zucchini and fresh cucumber strips get rolled up like sushi. Use any soft, spreadable cheese like Brie, fresh mozzarella, Boursin, Herbed Cream Cheese (page 66), or the goat cheese as prescribed.

Serves 4 to 6

3 medium-size zucchini, cut lengthwise into ¼-inch- (6.4 mm-) thick slices

Olive oil

Kosher salt and freshly ground black pepper

2 tomatoes, cut into wedges

Fresh basil leaves

1 pound (454 g) soft goat cheese

2 medium-size cucumbers, cut lengthwise into ¼-inch- (6.4 mm-) thick slices

Prepare a hot fire in your grill.

Lightly brush the zucchini slices with olive oil and season with salt and pepper. Grill one side of the zucchini for about 3 to 4 minutes, or until it gets good grill marks. Do not grill the other side.

On a platter, arrange the tomato wedges, season with salt and pepper, and top with some basil leaves. Assemble the roll-ups by lightly spreading goat cheese on the ungrilled sides of the zucchini strips and topping with a few basil leaves. Season the cucumber strips with salt and pepper, lightly spread with the goat cheese, and top with a few basil leaves. Then roll up each of the zucchini and cucumber strips and secure with a toothpick. Arrange all on the platter with the tomatoes.

Hot Diggity Dogs

This is our salute to hot dogs, all kinds, from ballpark franks to artisan sausages, cooked directly on the grill, smoked a bit, or cooked on a skewer. We have expanded beyond hot dogs to include a nod to our Germanic heritage with bratwurst, our Italian friends and their fennel-fragrant Italian sausages, and all the wonderful artisan butchers who create chicken-spinach-artichoke sausage combinations. If you don't like your hot dogs to get charred, try the hot dog roller racks that are available in grill stores.

CROSS-HATCHED HOT DOGS ON A STICK

Skewering and then slashing the hot dogs makes them cook really quickly, plus they look really cool. A chili sauce glaze makes them tasty.

Serves 4

4 large hot dogs, like ball-park franks

1 red onion

2 tablespoons unsalted butter, at room temperature

2 tablespoons mustard of your choice

4 good-quality bakery hot dog buns

¼ cup (57 g) chili sauce of your choice

1 garlic clove, minced

Prepare a hot fire in your grill.

Thread the hot dogs onto long metal or thick wooden skewers. Using a small knife, make spaced angled cuts down each side of the dogs. Do not slice all the way through.

Slice the onion into 3 thick slices and skewer the slices like lollipops on three separate skewers.

Combine the softened butter and mustard and spread on the cut sides of the buns. Combine the chili sauce and minced garlic in a small bowl for basting at the grill. Grill the buns, cut-side down, for about 30 seconds and then set aside on a plate.

The onions will take a bit longer to cook, about 3 minutes per side until charred, so start them next. When you turn the onions, start the hot dogs.

Set the hot dogs over the grill fire beside the onion lollipops. Grill the hot dogs, turning them every minute, for about 3 to 4 minutes, or until charred. Baste them with the chili and garlic sauce in the last minute of grilling. Slide the onions off the skewers and toss with tongs to separate the grilled rings.

Place a grilled hot dog in each bun, top with some grilled onion, and drizzle any remaining chili and garlic sauce over the top.

GRILLED BRATS *with* HORSERADISH BUTTER

Using foil packets is a very easy and clean way to grill. For those who like neat and tidy cooking, this method is for you. Mustard lovers will want to top their 'wursts with more, so have extra kinds of mustard on hand. Alternatively, you can always grill the brats directly over a medium-hot fire for 2 to 3 minutes every quarter turn, until they are cooked through and have good grill marks.

Serves 4

HORSERADISH BUTTER

$1/2$ cup (57 g) unsalted butter, at room temperature

$1^1/_2$ tablespoons freshly grated horseradish

1 teaspoon grainy mustard

GRILLED BRATS

4 good-quality bakery hot dog buns, or pumpernickel bread

4 bratwurst, knackwurst, or bockwurst sausages

2 cups (320 g) sauerkraut

1 yellow onion, sliced

Extra mustards of your choice, for serving

Marinated red pepper, sliced, for serving

Pickled jalapeño pepper, sliced, for serving

Prepare a medium-hot fire in your grill.

For the Horseradish Butter, combine the butter, horseradish, and mustard until well blended.

Lightly spread the butter mixture on the cut sides of the buns. Reserve any extra for another slather on the buns after they are grilled.

Grill the buns, cut-sides down, for about 30 seconds and then set aside on a plate. (If using pumpernickel bread, slather one side with the butter mixture and grill, butter-side down, for about 30 seconds; set aside.)

Place the brats in the center of an 18 x 12-inch (46 x 30 cm) doubled piece of heavy-duty foil. Top with the sauerkraut and sliced onion and close the packet. Place the foil packet seam-side up over the grill fire. Close the lid and grill for 15 to 20 minutes.

Be careful when you open the packet, as you will release the steam.

Serve the brats on the buns, topped with the sauerkraut and onion. Pass the extra mustard, red pepper strips, and jalapeños.

GRILLED ARTISAN SAUSAGES

The trick to these artisan sausages is to not have them break open while they are on the grill. So having a two-temperature grill works best. If the sausages are getting really good grill marks but are not quite done, move them to the low fire to let them continue to cook a little more. All the "hot dog" recipes can easily be doubled or tripled if you want to serve a crowd. And since the dogs are relatively small, there is room on the grill for ears of corn, too. With a great summer salad of greens or tomatoes, you have a tasty and colorful meal that is fairly simple to prepare. Buy the sausages at a meat counter that specializes in lots of different flavors, like Whole Foods Market or your favorite charcuterie maker.

Serves 4

4 bakery-fresh hoagie buns

Olive oil

4 artisan sausages, like chicken-artichoke, seafood, or Italian

Assorted condiments like mustards, aioli, tartar sauce, Mississippi Comeback Sauce (page 151), ketchup, BBQ sauce, and chili sauce

Assorted garnishes like lettuce, onions, pickles, olives, and tomatoes

Prepare a dual-heat fire in your grill with a low fire on one side and a medium-hot fire on the other side.

Slice the buns open, not quite cutting all the way through so that tops and bottoms are connected. Lightly brush the cut sides of the buns with olive oil. Grill the buns, cut-side down, for about 45 to 60 seconds over the medium-hot fire and then set aside on a plate.

Set the sausages on the medium-hot side of the grill and grill for about 2 minutes per quarter turn. If the sausages need more heat to char, continue to grill over the medium-hot side of the grill, continuing with a few more quarter turns. Then move the sausages to the low-heat side of the grill and grill for an additional 2 minutes per quarter turn, or until firm and done.

Serve the sausages on buns and pass the condiments and garnishes.

CHAPTER 3

Salads

AMERICANS HAVE HAD AN INTERESTING HISTORY WITH salad, from the salmagundi served in Colonial Williamsburg to the cabbage salads of Dutch and German immigrants to the not-a-vegetable-out-of-place gelatin salads so popular from the early 1920s onward. In the 1940s and '50s, the classic tossed or wedge salad featuring iceberg lettuce got a flavor assist from those now-iconic salad dressings: ranch, blue cheese, and green goddess.

And still we experiment.

Grilling greens, fruits, and vegetables adds a slightly smoky, caramelized flavor to salad, while still keeping the crunch. Each season, there is something wonderful to grill, from Grilled Romaine with Smoky Blue Cheese Dressing (page 93) in spring to Blistered Green Beans with Buttermilk Ranch Dressing (page 88) in summer, and Grilled Kale Bundles with Warm Cranberry-Bourbon Vinaigrette (page 94) in the fall and winter.

Salads celebrate every region—chiles in the Southwest, luscious pears in the Northwest, watermelon in the South, apples in the North, and fresh salad greens and vegetables from gardens everywhere.

Grilling doesn't have to be meat-centric anymore. One crisp and charry bite of Grilled Nectarines with Burrata and Orange Mint (page 91) should convince you.

We've included a few side salads and slaws that are not grilled and can be made ahead and kept in the refrigerator for a day or two: Quinoa, Feta, and Farm-Stand Vegetable Salad (page 98), Yankee Noodle Slaw (page 99), and Everything-in-the-Garden Pasta Salad (page 100).

★ ★ ★

**Grilled Peaches, Country Ham,
and Frisée with Sorghum Drizzle**

**Grilled Radicchio Wedges
with Green Goddess Dressing**

**Grilled Onion, Pepper, and Corn Salad
with Cilantro Lime Vinaigrette**

Grilled Fingerling Potato Salad with Hot Bacon Dressing

**Grilled Pear, Hazelnut, and Mint Salad
with Charry Lemon Vinaigrette**

**Grilled Watermelon and Tomato Salad
with Hot Pepper Jelly Vinaigrette**

**Blistered Green Beans
with Buttermilk Ranch Dressing**

Grill-Roasted Red Pepper, Feta, and Chives

Grilled Nectarines with Burrata and Orange Mint

Grilled Zucchini with Ricotta Salata and Dill

Grill-Roasted Cherry Tomatoes with Mozzarella and Basil

Grilled Romaine with Smoky Blue Cheese Dressing

**Grilled Kale Bundles with
Warm Cranberry-Bourbon Vinaigrette**

Garden Tomatoes with Grilled White Cheddar Corn Sticks

Quinoa, Feta, and Farm-Stand Vegetable Salad

Yankee Noodle Slaw

Everything-in-the-Garden Pasta Salad

★ ★ ★

GRILLED PEACHES, COUNTRY HAM, AND FRISÉE *with* SORGHUM DRIZZLE

Sweet and salty flavors come together in this Kentucky salad. If country ham is not available in your area, use prosciutto instead; you can also use local wildflower honey or pure cane syrup in place of sorghum. Adapted from a recipe by Levon Wallace of Proof on Main in Louisville, Kentucky.

Serves 4 to 6

4 large ripe, firm peaches, pitted and halved

12 thin slices country ham or prosciutto (about 12 ounces /340 g)

Olive oil, for brushing

Freshly ground black pepper

2 small heads frisée or other frilly, bitter green, torn

1/2 cup (120 ml) sorghum

Prepare a medium-hot fire in your grill.

Cut each peach half into thirds. Wrap each third with a slice of ham and secure with toothpicks. Transfer the peach wedges to a large baking sheet to carry out to the grill. Brush with olive oil and season with pepper.

Grill each peach wedge for 3 minutes, turning often, until the ham turns a dark pink and looks caramelized.

To serve, line a platter with frisée. Top with the grilled, ham-wrapped peach wedges. Drizzle with sorghum and serve.

GRILLED RADICCHIO WEDGES
with GREEN GODDESS DRESSING

Grilling cabbage wedges give you the crunch of a salad with the flavor of the grill. The hearty radicchio—or small wedges of red or napa cabbage—stands up to the bold flavor of the classic green goddess dressing, created by Philip Roemer at the Palace Hotel in San Francisco in 1923. The colors in this salad look like an early Technicolor movie. You will have extra dressing; it is also good on grilled shrimp or fish, chicken, or other vegetables.

Serves 6

GREEN GODDESS DRESSING

8 to 10 anchovy fillets

1 green onion, chopped (white part with some of the green)

2 garlic cloves, minced

$\frac{1}{2}$ cup (120 ml) tarragon vinegar or rice wine vinegar

$\frac{1}{4}$ cup (11 g) minced fresh parsley

$\frac{1}{2}$ cup (21 g) finely snipped fresh chives

3 cups (680 g) mayonnaise

GRILLED RADICCHIO

6 heads radicchio, outer leaves trimmed and stems intact

Olive oil, for brushing

Kosher salt and freshly ground black pepper

For the Green Goddess Dressing, mash the anchovy fillets, green onion, and garlic together with a fork in a medium bowl until you have a paste. Stir in the vinegar and then the parsley and chives. Whisk in the mayonnaise. Cover and chill until ready to serve. Keeps in the refrigerator for up to 3 days.

Prepare a hot fire in your grill.

Cut each radicchio head in half lengthwise. Brush the cut sides with olive oil and season with salt and pepper. Place on a large baking sheet to take out to the grill.

Grill the radicchio, cut-side down, for 2 to 3 minutes, or until you have good grill marks.

To serve, place 2 radicchio halves on each salad plate and dollop with the Green Goddess Dressing.

GRILLED ONION, PEPPER, AND CORN SALAD *with* CILANTRO LIME VINAIGRETTE

With Southwest style and farm-fresh flavor, this colorful salad makes perfect platter food. The chipotle chile in the vinaigrette is a ripened jalapeño pepper smoked over pecan wood. Cotija is a dry Mexican grating cheese similar to Romano or Parmesan. If you like, serve grilled chicken, fish, or burgers on the side.

Serves 4

CILANTRO LIME VINAIGRETTE

1 cup (42 g) coarsely chopped cilantro leaves and tender stems

1 canned chipotle chile in adobo sauce

1 large garlic clove, roughly chopped

⅓ cup (80 ml) rice wine vinegar

⅓ cup (80 ml) freshly squeezed lime juice

2 tablespoons honey

⅔ cup (160 ml) vegetable oil

Kosher salt

SALAD

2 large red onions, thickly sliced

1 pound (454 g) Anaheim, shishito, or other small, somewhat-sweet peppers

4 ears fresh corn, shucked

Olive oil, for brushing

Kosher salt and freshly ground black pepper

½ cup (113 g) crumbled Cotija or grated Parmesan cheese

For the Cilantro Lime Vinaigrette, combine the cilantro, chile, garlic, vinegar, lime juice, honey, and oil in a food processor or high-speed blender and process until emulsified. Season with salt to taste. Use right away or transfer to a jar with a lid. The vinaigrette will keep in the refrigerator for up to 1 week.

Prepare a medium-hot fire in your grill. Place the onion slices, peppers, and ears of corn on a large baking sheet to prepare the vegetables. Brush the vegetables with olive oil and season with salt and pepper.

Grill the onions for about 8 minutes, turning once halfway through, or until softened and slightly charred. Grill the peppers for about 5 minutes, turning once, until they have puffed up and blistered. Grill the corn for about 5 minutes, turning a quarter turn every minute or so, until the kernels have grill marks.

To serve, arrange overlapping onion slices and the whole peppers on a platter. With a sharp knife, cut the grilled corn off the cob into planks and arrange on the platter. Drizzle with the vinaigrette and sprinkle with Cotija.

GRILLED FINGERLING POTATO SALAD *with* HOT BACON DRESSING

German communities throughout the Midwest love their tangy potato salad and trusty applewood-smoked bacon from Nueske's in Wisconsin, Nodine's in Connecticut, or Pine Street Market in Georgia; hickory-smoked bacon from Benton's Smoky Mountain Country Ham in Tennessee; or white-oak smoked bacon from Claus' German Sausage and Meat in Indiana. Grilling the potatoes instead of boiling them adds even more flavor. You can serve this salad hot off the grill, or grill the potatoes a day ahead and serve the salad at room temperature. If you want (vegan) smoky flavor without the bacon, try dressing this salad with Smoked Cashew Crema (page 72) instead of the Hot Bacon Dressing.

Serves 8

POTATO SALAD

2 pounds (1 kg) fingerling potatoes

Olive oil

Kosher salt and freshly ground black pepper

6 to 8 green onions, chopped (white part with some of the green)

HOT BACON DRESSING

4 slices thick-cut smoked bacon, chopped

$1/2$ cup (120 ml) cider vinegar

3 tablespoons (44 ml) balsamic vinegar

3 tablespoons (44 ml) water

$1^1/2$ teaspoons granulated sugar

1 teaspoon kosher salt

$1/2$ teaspoon ground white pepper

$1/2$ teaspoon celery seed

Prepare a hot fire in your grill.

On a large baking sheet, drizzle the fingerling potatoes with olive oil and season with salt and pepper.

Grill the fingerlings in a perforated grill basket or an aluminum pan with holes in it. Place over the hot fire and close the grill lid. After about 3 to 4 minutes, open the grill and toss the potatoes. Close the lid again, cook for 3 to 4 minutes, and toss again. Cook until the potatoes are tender when pierced with a fork.

Transfer the potatoes to a large bowl.

For the Hot Bacon Dressing, fry the bacon in a medium skillet until crisp. Add the vinegars and water and heat until boiling. Lower the heat to medium and stir in the sugar, salt, white pepper, and celery seed, stirring well for 2 to 3 minutes, or until the sugar dissolves. Pour the hot dressing over the grilled fingerlings and top with the chopped green onion. Serve warm.

GRILLED PEAR, HAZELNUT, AND MINT SALAD *with* CHARRY LEMON VINAIGRETTE

The Pacific Northwest is rightly famous for its juicy pears and crisp hazelnuts, which come together in this salad bowl. Cooking the quinoa in pear nectar, available bottled, gives this dish a double-whammy of pear flavor—plus the vegan protein is plenty filling.

Serves 4 to 6

PEAR SALAD

1 cup (227 g) white quinoa

2 cups (480 ml) pear nectar

4 firm, ripe pears, peeled, cored, and quartered

Olive oil, for brushing

1 lemon

6 to 8 green onions, sliced (white part with some of the green)

1/4 cup (11 g) packed finely chopped fresh mint leaves

1/3 cup (77 g) toasted hazelnuts

CHARRY LEMON VINAIGRETTE

Juice of 1 grilled lemon (see above)

Grated zest of 1 lemon (see above)

1 tablespoon rice wine vinegar

1 teaspoon Dijon mustard

1 teaspoon sorghum or maple syrup

1/4 cup (60 ml) olive oil

Kosher salt and freshly ground black pepper

For the salad, combine the quinoa and pear nectar in a saucepan over medium-high heat. Bring to a boil, reduce the heat, cover, and simmer for 15 to 20 minutes, or until the quinoa is tender. Add a little water during cooking, if necessary. Remove from the heat, keep covered, and let rest for 5 minutes. Remove the lid, fluff with a fork, and divide among 4 to 6 individual salad bowls.

Prepare a medium-hot fire in your grill.

Brush the pear wedges with olive oil and grill for 4 to 5 minutes, turning often, until the pears have good grill marks. Zest the lemon and set the zest aside for the dressing. Halve the lemon and grill, cut-side down, for 1 to 2 minutes, or until it has good grill marks; set aside for the dressing.

Place the grilled pear, green onions, mint, and hazelnuts on top of each bowl of quinoa.

For the Charry Lemon Vinaigrette, juice the grilled lemon halves into a bowl. Whisk in the lemon zest, vinegar, mustard, sorghum, and olive oil until well blended. Season with salt and pepper. Spoon the vinaigrette over each bowl and serve.

GRILLED WATERMELON
AND TOMATO SALAD *with*
HOT PEPPER JELLY VINAIGRETTE

There's a way to grill everything, even watermelon. Adapted from a recipe by New Orleans chef John Besh, this sweet salad tastes great hot from the grill on a summer's day. Experiment and try substituting cantaloupe or honeydew instead of the watermelon. Keeping the rind on the melon makes it easy to hold together and turn on the grill.

Serves 6 to 8

HOT PEPPER
JELLY VINAIGRETTE

$^1\!/_2$ cup (113 g) hot red pepper jelly

$^1\!/_2$ cup (120 ml) red wine vinegar

1 teaspoon sambal chili paste (found in the Asian section of the grocery store)

$1^1\!/_2$ cups (360 ml) vegetable oil

$^1\!/_2$ teaspoon kosher salt

GRILLED WATERMELON
AND TOMATO SALAD

6 thick slices seedless red or yellow watermelon, with the rind on

12 Roma tomatoes, halved lengthwise

3 cups (127 g) baby lettuces

1 (8-ounce/226 g) container small fresh mozzarella balls or bocconcini, drained

12 fresh basil leaves, torn, for garnish

For the Hot Pepper Jelly Vinaigrette, whisk the pepper jelly, vinegar, chili paste, oil, and salt together in a bowl until emulsified. Set aside or transfer to a jar with a lid and refrigerate for up to 1 week.

Prepare a hot fire in your grill.

Brush the cut sides of the watermelon and tomatoes with some of the vinaigrette. Place them on a large baking sheet to take outside, and reserve the remaining vinaigrette.

Place the watermelon slices and tomatoes, cut-side down, on the grill and grill for 4 to 5 minutes, turning once, until the watermelon has some grill marks and the tomatoes have caramelized. Transfer to the baking sheet.

To serve, arrange the baby lettuces on a platter. Cut the watermelon into bite-size pieces, discarding the rind. Arrange the watermelon, tomatoes, and mozzarella on the greens and spoon over the remaining vinaigrette. Garnish with the basil leaves.

BLISTERED GREEN BEANS
with BUTTERMILK RANCH DRESSING

We could make a meal on this alone. But it's also mighty fine with grilled or planked salmon or a ranch hand's favorite—a juicy steak. We like to serve this in a bowl or on a platter—it's so much tastier and more unexpected than slaw or potato salad. You will have more Buttermilk Ranch Dressing than you strictly need for this salad, but it keeps in the refrigerator. And kids of all ages love it—with or without grilled veggies to dip in it.

Serves 6

BUTTERMILK RANCH DRESSING

3 green onions, chopped (white part with some green)

¹/₂ cup (21 g) torn fresh basil leaves

2 tablespoons freshly squeezed lemon juice

1 tablespoon Dijon mustard

1 tablespoon olive oil

2 large garlic cloves, roughly chopped

1 cup (227 g) mayonnaise

¹/₂ cup (113 g) nonfat Greek yogurt

¹/₂ cup (120 ml) buttermilk

Kosher salt and freshly ground black pepper

BLISTERED GREEN BEANS

1¹/₂ pounds (680 g) fresh slender green beans

1 tablespoon olive oil

1 tablespoon Cajun seasoning, barbecue rub of your choice, or Blackening Spice Rub (page 32)

For the Buttermilk Ranch Dressing, place the green onions, basil, lemon juice, mustard, olive oil, and garlic in a food processor fitted with a steel blade. Process the mixture for 30 seconds, or until the ingredients are puréed. Add the mayonnaise, yogurt, and buttermilk and process again until well blended. Season with salt and pepper. Transfer to a large container, cover, and refrigerate for at least 1 hour before serving. Keeps in the refrigerator for up to 1 week.

Prepare a hot fire in your grill.

In a bowl, toss the beans with the olive oil to coat, then sprinkle on the seasoning and toss again. Transfer the beans to a grill basket or a grill wok set on a large baking sheet to transport to the grill.

Place the grill basket or grill wok directly over the fire. Turn the grill basket from time to time or stir-grill by tossing the beans with wooden paddles or grill spatulas until tender and blistered, about 8 to 10 minutes.

To serve, transfer the beans to a platter and spoon over the dressing.

→ A SIDE OF RANCH ←

It seems like we've always had ranch dressing, doesn't it? But it didn't appear on the American culinary landscape until the 1950s. Kenneth "Steve" Henson, a Nebraska cowboy, headed northwest in 1949 to make his fortune in Alaska. There wasn't gold, but there was plumbing, so he became a plumbing contractor working in the bush. Part of his job was cooking for fellow workers, and he created this recipe. In 1954, he and his wife, Gayle, opened a dude ranch in California, which they named Hidden Valley Ranch. They served this dressing. It became popular, so they started making extra and selling it to their guests, both as a prepared dressing and as a dry seasoning mix to add to mayonnaise and buttermilk. The rest is history.

RAZZLE DAZZLE CAPRESE, FOUR WAYS

Insalata Caprese (Salad of Capri) makes the most of Italy's best ingredients: sun-kissed tomatoes, fragrant basil, creamy buffalo mozzarella, fresh olive oil, and a little salt and pepper. That's it. We've taken the caprese formula and translated it to the American grill to create "can you believe they're this easy?" salads. Of course, you want the best and freshest ingredients for the most delicious results. Try one version, and then change it up the next time. Any of these salads are delicious on grilled bread.

Serves 4

GRILL-ROASTED RED PEPPER, FETA, AND CHIVES

2 large red bell peppers

Olive oil

Kosher salt and freshly ground black pepper

8 ounces (227 g) feta cheese in a block, drained and cut into 8 slices

2 tablespoons coarsely snipped fresh chives, or more to taste

★ ★ ★

GRILLED NECTARINES WITH BURRATA AND ORANGE MINT

2 large fresh nectarines, halved and pitted

Olive oil

8 ounces (227 g) burrata cheese, drained and cut into 8 slices

Kosher salt and freshly ground black pepper

4 (6-inch/15 cm) sprigs fresh orange mint

★ ★ ★

GRILLED ZUCCHINI WITH RICOTTA SALATA AND DILL

2 large green zucchini, ends trimmed, cut into long, 1-inch- (2.5 cm-) thick slices

Olive oil

8 ounces (227 g) ricotta salata cheese in a block,

drained and cut into 8 slices
Kosher salt and freshly ground black pepper
4 (6-inch/15 cm) sprigs fresh dill

★ ★ ★

GRILL-ROASTED CHERRY TOMATOES
WITH MOZZARELLA AND BASIL

2 pints (900 g) cherry tomatoes
Olive oil
8 ounces (227 g) fresh mozzarella cheese, cut into 8 slices
Kosher salt and freshly ground black pepper
24 fresh basil leaves

Prepare a medium-hot fire in your grill.

For Grill-Roasted Red Pepper, Feta, and Chives, brush the whole red peppers with olive oil and place over direct heat. Grill, turning every few minutes, until the peppers have good grill marks all over. Remove the peppers from the grill and place them in a paper or plastic bag, close the bag, and let them steam until they're cool enough to handle. Brush off some of the charred bits, if you like. Then stem, seed, and cut each pepper into 8 slices. To serve, place 2 slices of red pepper on each plate and season lightly with salt and pepper, and then add 2 slices of feta. Drizzle with olive oil and sprinkle with chives.

For Grilled Nectarines with Burrata and Orange Mint, brush the nectarine halves with olive oil. Grill the nectarine halves, cut-side down, for 2 to 3 minutes, or until you have good grill marks. Remove the nectarines from the grill and slice each nectarine half into 3 slices. To serve, arrange 3 nectarine slices and 2 slices of burrata on each plate and season with salt and pepper. Drizzle with olive oil and garnish with an orange mint sprig.

For Grilled Zucchini with Ricotta Salata and Dill, brush each zucchini slice with olive oil. Grill for 2 to 3 minutes on one side, or until you have good grill marks. Remove from the grill. To serve, divide the zucchini slices among 4 plates, add 2 slices of ricotta salata to each, and season with salt and pepper. Drizzle with olive oil and add a sprig of dill.

For Grill-Roasted Cherry Tomatoes with Mozzarella and Basil, place the cherry tomatoes in a disposable aluminum pan, drizzle with olive oil, and gently toss to coat. Grill, covered, for 10 minutes, stirring occasionally, until the cherry tomatoes have softened. Divide the grilled cherry tomatoes among 4 plates, add 2 slices of mozzarella to each, and season with salt and pepper. Drizzle with more olive oil and garnish with basil leaves.

GRILLED ROMAINE WITH
SMOKY BLUE CHEESE DRESSING

Grilled romaine has become a cult favorite, and for good reason. It's delicious. So, we're always looking for ways to make it fresh again. Here is a new spin on grilled romaine, the wedge salad, and classic blue cheese dressing, all in one. The smoked blue cheese adds to the bacony flavor. Use a smoked blue cheese such as Salemville's applewood smoked blue cheese from Wisconsin, hazelnut shell–smoked blue from Oregon's Rogue Creamery, or fruitwood-smoked blue from Roth Kase, also in Wisconsin.

Serves 8

SMOKY BLUE CHEESE DRESSING

$^1/_2$ cup (115 g) mayonnaise

$^1/_2$ cup (115 g) nonfat Greek yogurt

4 ounces (113 g) smoked blue cheese, crumbled

1 teaspoon Worcestershire sauce

Freshly ground black pepper

GRILLED ROMAINE

4 hearts of romaine, halved lengthwise, rinsed and drained on towels

Olive oil, for brushing

Kosher salt and freshly ground black pepper

1 pound (454 g) sliced bacon, cooked crisp and crumbled

1 pint (310 g) cherry tomatoes, halved

For the Smoky Blue Cheese Dressing, whisk the mayonnaise, yogurt, smoked blue cheese, and Worcestershire sauce together in a bowl and season with pepper. Keeps in the refrigerator for a week.

Prepare a hot fire in your grill.

Brush the cut sides of the romaine with olive oil and season with salt and pepper.

Grill the greens with the cut sides down for about 2 to 3 minutes, or until browned with good grill marks. (Do not close the grill lid.)

To serve, arrange half a romaine heart on each plate and dollop with Smoky Blue Cheese Dressing. Sprinkle the crumbled bacon over the lettuce and garnish with the cherry tomatoes.

GRILLED KALE BUNDLES *with* WARM CRANBERRY-BOURBON VINAIGRETTE

Hearty greens like kale take well to the grill. Switch out the wire tie on bunched green Lacinato kale, also known as dinosaur or dino kale, for twine and you're good to go. With a Parmesan baste during cooking and a finish of tart cranberry, this knife-and-fork salad will persuade you that kale is still a star.

Serves 4

KALE BUNDLES

2 (8-ounce/227 g) bunches
   fresh kale

¹/₂ cup (120 ml) olive oil

¹/₂ cup (113 g) finely grated
   Parmesan or Romano cheese

WARM CRANBERRY-BOURBON VINAIGRETTE

1 cup (115 g) fresh cranberries

¹/₂ cup (113 g) granulated sugar

¹/₄ cup (60 ml) cider vinegar

¹/₄ cup (60 ml) freshly squeezed
   orange juice

¹/₄ cup (60 ml) vegetable oil

¹/₂ teaspoon red pepper flakes

¹/₂ teaspoon ground cinnamon

¹/₂ teaspoon garlic salt

2 tablespoons bourbon

Prepare a medium-hot fire in your grill.

For the Kale Bundles, divide each bunch in half and tie together again with kitchen twine, about 1 inch (2.5 cm) from the stem ends.

Combine the olive oil and Parmesan in a bowl. Place the kale on a large baking sheet and brush with some of the Parmesan mixture.

For the Warm Cranberry-Bourbon Vinaigrette, bring the cranberries, sugar, and vinegar to a boil in a medium saucepan over medium-high heat, and cook until the cranberries pop, about 5 to 7 minutes. Stir in the orange juice, vegetable oil, pepper flakes, cinnamon, garlic salt, and bourbon and set aside.

Grill the kale with the grill lid closed, turning often and basting with the Parmesan mixture, until the greens have browned on all sides and have slightly wilted, about 8 minutes.

To serve, spoon the vinaigrette on 4 salad plates and set the kale bunches on the dressing.

GARDEN TOMATOES *with* GRILLED
WHITE CHEDDAR CORN STICKS

This is pure summer! A platter of tomatoes cut into slices and wedges, perhaps all different kinds from your garden or farmers' market, including little red and yellow teardrops or cherries. A scattering of Grilled Corn Sticks laced with some Wisconsin white Cheddar cheese is a crunchy alternative to croutons. Drizzled with the Fresh Herb Vinaigrette, this is so fresh and vibrant, you'll serve it again and again. The cornmeal mixture needs to be made at least 4 hours in advance and refrigerated until it is firm. It can be made a day or two ahead as well.

Serves 6 to 8

GRILLED CORN STICKS

2 1/4 cups (540 ml) water

3/4 cup (117 g) cornmeal

1/2 teaspoon kosher salt

1/4 cup (28 g) unsalted butter, plus more for the pan

2 ounces (56 g) aged white Cheddar cheese, grated

Olive oil, for brushing

FRESH HERB VINAIGRETTE

1 cup (240 ml) vegetable oil

1/2 cup (80 ml) white wine vinegar

2 tablespoons freshly squeezed lemon juice

1 tablespoon minced fresh thyme, basil, or chives

1 tablespoon finely chopped red onion

1 1/2 teaspoons Dijon mustard

1/2 teaspoon kosher salt

For the Grilled Corn Sticks, in a large saucepan, bring the water to a boil and slowly whisk in the cornmeal so that it doesn't clump together. Add the salt and continue to cook over medium heat for about 5 minutes; the mixture will be stiff. Turn off the heat and whisk in the butter and cheese. Let cool for about 5 minutes and then pour the batter into an 8 x 8-inch (20 x 20 cm) buttered pan. Refrigerate for at least 4 hours.

For the Fresh Herb Vinaigrette, combine all the ingredients in a large glass jar, cover with the lid, and shake to combine. Keeps in the refrigerator for 2 to 3 days.

Oil the grill grates and then prepare a medium-hot fire in your grill.

Run a knife around the edges of the cornmeal mixture to loosen. Turn the pan upside down on top of a cutting board covered with oiled foil. The cornmeal should be in one piece. Cut the cornmeal into sticks that are easy to handle on the grill, about 1 x 4-inch (2.5 x 10 cm) pieces. You should have 16 sticks. Slide the foil onto a baking sheet for carrying out to the grill and liberally brush the sticks with olive oil. Grill the sticks for 3 to 4 minutes on each side, or until they have good grill marks and are easy to turn. Set aside.

Slice and quarter the tomatoes and halve some of the

GARDEN TOMATOES

2 pounds (1 kg) tomatoes,
assorted varieties, shapes,
and colors

1 pint (284 g) teardrop and/or
cherry tomatoes

Kosher salt and freshly ground
black pepper

teardrop and cherry tomatoes. Lightly salt the tomatoes.

To serve, arrange the tomatoes and corn sticks on a platter. Top the salad with freshly ground pepper and drizzle with some of the vinaigrette.

QUINOA, FETA, *and* FARM-STAND VEGETABLE SALAD

Quinoa makes this a healthy grain side salad. While the quinoa cooks (about 12 minutes), you can grill the lemon halves and chop all the vegetables. Celery adds a nice crunch to this salad: don't hesitate to chop up the celery tops, leaves and all, for a refreshing addition. Serve the salad immediately at room temperature or chill it. It can be prepared a couple days beforehand and refrigerated. If doing so, save the feta to add right before serving. Change it to a pasta salad if you like, using cooked orzo pasta instead of the quinoa.

Serves 8

2 cups (480 ml) water

1 cup (227 g) quinoa

1 teaspoon kosher salt

2 lemons, halved

⅓ cup (80 ml) olive oil

4 to 6 green onions, thinly sliced (white and green parts)

1 to 2 cucumbers, seeded and diced

½ cup (22 g) chopped celery stem and tops with leaves

2 tablespoons chopped fresh flat-leaf parsley

2 tablespoons chopped Kalamata olives, or more to taste

1½ cups (340 g) crumbled feta cheese

In a saucepan, bring the water to a boil. Add the quinoa and salt. Cover the pan and simmer over medium heat for about 12 minutes. Turn off the heat and let the quinoa sit, covered, for about 5 minutes.

Prepare a hot fire in your grill. Place the lemon halves directly over the fire, cut side down, and grill for about 3 to 4 minutes, or until charred.

Drain the liquid from the quinoa, if any, and place it in a medium bowl. Squeeze the grilled lemons over the quinoa, add the olive oil, and stir to blend. Stir in the green onions, cucumbers, celery, parsley, and olives.

If serving immediately, fold in the crumbled feta. Otherwise, refrigerate the salad and add the feta right before serving.

YANKEE NOODLE SLAW

What's so American about ramen noodles? Only that they are everywhere in the U.S., from ramen noodle shops (restaurants) to grocery stores, where bulk buys of 10 to 20 flavored packages of ramen noodles make for very inexpensive quick-fix meals. When these Asian noodles came to our shores after World War II, many tasty variations of Asian-style salads and slaws appeared at ladies luncheons and on summer dinner tables. Here is our take on this retro classic, which pairs beautifully with grilled pork tenderloin or chicken marinated in our Toasted Sesame Dressing (page 100).

Serves 6 to 8

1 (3-ounce/85 g) package uncooked chicken-flavored ramen noodles

¼ cup (57 g) unsalted butter

½ cup dry-roasted shelled sunflower seeds

1 large head napa cabbage, shredded

6 green onions, chopped (white and green parts)

¼ cup (60 ml) vegetable oil

¼ cup (60 ml) cider vinegar

1 tablespoon soy sauce

1 tablespoon toasted sesame oil

2 tablespoons granulated sugar

Crush the noodles into bite-size pieces. Melt the butter in a medium skillet over medium heat. Cook the noodles until they are browned then add the sunflower seeds, stirring often to prevent burning. Remove the skillet from the heat, let it cool, and transfer the noodles to a large bowl. Add the cabbage and green onions, tossing to combine.

Prepare the dressing by whisking together the vegetable oil, cider vinegar, soy sauce, sesame oil, and sugar. Pour over the salad, toss, and serve.

EVERYTHING-IN-THE-GARDEN PASTA SALAD

Pasta salads are great make-ahead sides that go with just about any grilled meats. This pasta side gets its depth of flavor from the soy and toasted sesame oil. You can add anything from your garden: peas, green beans, cucumbers, peppers, tomatoes, celery, radishes, and more.

Serves 6 to 8

PASTA SALAD

8 ounces (227 g) thin spaghetti

Kosher salt

Extra-virgin olive oil

4 ounces (113 g) bean sprouts

2 cucumbers, seeded and chopped

1 (8-ounce/227 g) package coleslaw mix

1 red bell pepper, seeded and thinly sliced

12 cherry tomatoes, halved

8 green onions, chopped (white and green parts)

3 stalks celery, sliced

1 bunch fresh cilantro, chopped

2 cups (250 g) roasted and salted peanuts, chopped

TOASTED SESAME DRESSING

$^2/_3$ cup (160 ml) vegetable oil

$^1/_3$ cup (80 ml) soy sauce

$^1/_3$ cup (80 ml) rice wine vinegar

2 tablespoons toasted sesame oil

$^1/_4$ cup (57 g) packed light brown sugar

2 tablespoons peeled and chopped fresh ginger

2 garlic cloves, chopped

Cook the spaghetti in a large pot of salted boiling water according to the package directions (add about a tablespoon of extra-virgin olive oil to the water before adding the pasta). Reserve 1 cup (240 ml) of the pasta water. Drain the pasta, place it in a large bowl and let it cool. Add the bean sprouts, cucumbers, slaw, pepper, tomatoes, green onions, celery, cilantro, and peanuts and toss together.

For the Toasted Sesame Dressing, combine all the ingredients in a bowl and whisk together until blended. Pour the dressing over the salad and mix together using tongs or your clean hands. If the salad seems a bit dry, add some of the reserved pasta water as needed. Serve in a bowl immediately at room temperature or cover and refrigerate for several hours before serving.

CHAPTER 4

Big Bowls, Plates, and Party Platters

LET'S CELEBRATE OUR INDEPENDENCE FROM INDOOR-ONLY cooking. From Maine lobster to Texas-style brisket, Alaskan wild-caught salmon to Midwestern farm chicken, all we need is fire and smoke to make it taste really great. And it just makes sense to serve grilled or smoked foods in a casual style—in big, unbreakable bowls, or on plates and party platters.

Classic dishes like Grill-Roasted Shrimp and Smoked Garlic Grits (page 106) love the grill. And if you ever want to capture the flavor of a steakhouse steak—that charry crust, that buttery deliciousness—you can try Cast-Iron Cowboy Steak with Bacon Bourbon Butter (page 119). You don't have to live by the ocean to enjoy a Shore Dinner on the Grill (page 109) or Grilled Mahi-Mahi with Macadamia Butter (page 115).

You can also travel to the Southwest by taste buds with Piquillo Pepper–Stuffed Chicken Breasts with Green Olive Tapenade (page 133) and Corn Husk–Wrapped Turkey Breast with Hatch Chiles and Monterey Jack (page 137). Or head to your favorite trout stream for Oak-Grilled Trout with Campfire Potatoes (page 114).

Of course, we give ample space for tried-and-true, slow-smoked recipes, too. The Texas-Style Brisket in a Bag (page 122) is tender and smoky. The Double-Smoked Kentucky Ham with Apricot BBQ Sauce (page 127) is simple and perfect for any holiday table or for when a big crowd gathers. We marvel at how fantastic the Cherry Chipotle Barbecue Sauce is in our Cherry Chipotle Pork Butt recipe (page 128). Our flavor twist on ribs is unique, with a Root Beer Rib Rub and a Root Beer Glaze to make Root Beer Ribs (page 125)—suds up!

There's a great dish in this chapter for weeknight meals, weekend get-togethers, rainy days, sunny days, and everything in between.

★ ★ ★

Char-Grilled Tomato and Red Bell Pepper Soup

Grill-Roasted Shrimp and Smoked Garlic Grits

Big Bowl of Mussels with Grilled Potato Dippers

Shore Dinner on the Grill

Planked Salmon with Smoky
Orange Aioli and Salsa Verde

Whitefish with Horseradish Sauce and a Kiss of Smoke

Cast-Iron Scallops with Browned Lemon Butter and Chives

Oak-Grilled Trout with Campfire Potatoes

Grilled Mahi-Mahi with Macadamia Butter

Mesquite-Smoked Bison Chili

Sirloin with Wild Mushroom Grilling Paste

Cast-Iron Cowboy Steak with Bacon Bourbon Butter

Creole Coffee-Rubbed Beef Tenderloin

Texas-Style Brisket in a Bag

Root Beer Ribs

Double-Smoked Ham with Apricot BBQ Sauce

Cherry Chipotle Pork Butt

Sesame-Soy Marinated Pork Tenderloin
with Smoked Applesauce

Planked Chicken Breasts with Chile Lime Sofrito

Piquillo Pepper–Stuffed Chicken Breasts with Green Olive Tapenade

Sizzling Wings with Hot Sage Butter and Romano

Grilled Chicken Spiedini with Fresh Basil Cream Sauce

Corn Husk–Wrapped Turkey Breast
with Hatch Chiles and Monterey Jack

★ ★ ★

CHAR-GRILLED TOMATO
and RED BELL PEPPER SOUP

"Grill once, eat twice" is a motto we live by. When you grill extra vegetables—easy to do when you have a big harvest from your garden or from the farmers' market—you have leftovers that can go into great dishes like this one. We especially love the jaunty flourish of crumbled bacon, crumbled feta, and snipped chives, a wavy banner of deliciousness across the top of the soup.

Serves 4

- 2 large beefsteak tomatoes, thickly sliced
- 1 red bell pepper, stemmed, seeded, and halved lengthwise
- 1 medium-size red onion, thickly sliced
- ¼ cup (60 ml) olive oil, plus more for brushing
- 2 tablespoons red wine vinegar
- 1 tablespoon Worcestershire sauce
- ½ teaspoon kosher salt
- ½ teaspoon hot pepper sauce
- 4 slices bacon, cooked until crisp and crumbled
- 4 ounces (113 g) feta cheese, crumbled
- 2 tablespoons snipped fresh chives

Prepare a hot fire in your grill. Brush the tomatoes, bell pepper, and onions with some olive oil. Grill for 8 to 10 minutes, turning once, or until the tomatoes have some char but are still firm and the peppers and onions are nicely charred on all sides. Transfer the grilled vegetables to a food processor or blender and pulse until finely chopped. Add the ¼ cup (60 ml) olive oil, vinegar, Worcestershire, salt, and hot pepper sauce and purée until smooth. Serve immediately or refrigerate until chilled, reheating if you like: this soup is good served hot or cold.

To serve, ladle the soup into bowls and then top with wavy lines of crumbled bacon, feta, and chives to make a banner.

GRILL-ROASTED SHRIMP
and SMOKED GARLIC GRITS

Shrimp and grits deserve to go in the American culinary hall of fame. We've hardly met a version we didn't like, but this one has the flavor of the grill and the smoker. If you don't have smoked garlic on hand, you can cheat with a little drop or two of liquid smoke flavoring. Grill-roasting the shrimp and bacon together delivers big flavor, plump shrimp, and the mess left outside. We started with the recipe blueprint from Bill Smith of Crook's Corner in Chapel Hill, North Carolina, and went from there. Coarse grits take about 45 minutes to cook; our favorites include those by Anson Mills in Columbia, South Carolina, and Virginia Willis: My Southern Pantry, both available online.

Serves 4

SMOKED GARLIC GRITS

2 cups (480 ml) whole milk

2 cups (480 ml) water

1 cup (170 g) stone-ground coarse grits

2 tablespoons unsalted butter, divided

½ teaspoon kosher salt

½ teaspoon freshly ground black pepper

1 head puréed smoke-roasted garlic (see page 167), or 2 garlic cloves, minced, plus 1 teaspoon bottled liquid smoke flavoring

GRILL-ROASTED SHRIMP, BACON, AND TOMATOES

1¼ pounds (567 g) headless large (21 to 25 count) peeled and deveined shrimp

For the Smoked Garlic Grits, pour the milk and water into a large saucepan, cover, and turn the heat to medium high. When the liquid simmers, slowly add the grits while constantly whisking, then add 1 tablespoon of the butter and the salt and reduce the heat to medium. (If you pour the grits into the pan too fast, they will clump.) Cook, stirring every couple of minutes, until the grits have become fragrant and are the consistency of thick soup, about 15 minutes. Reduce the heat to low and simmer, stirring often (more frequently than before), for about 25 minutes, by which time the bubbles will emerge infrequently, as the grits have stiffened and fall lazily from the end of a spoon. Add the black pepper and garlic and cook for about 20 minutes more, stirring constantly to prevent the thickened grits from scorching on the bottom of the pan. If your grits thicken too quickly, or if they are too gritty for your taste, add water by the ½ cup, stirring to incorporate, and continue cooking until tender. Finish with the remaining tablespoon of butter. Assign another person to stir the grits while they finish, and go outside to the grill.

Prepare an indirect fire in your grill, with a hot fire on one side and no fire on the other. Combine the

4 ounces (113 g) slab bacon, cut into small dice and cooked until crisp

1 pound (454 g) Roma tomatoes, halved lengthwise

Olive oil, for brushing

1 teaspoon red wine vinegar, or more to taste

1/2 teaspoon kosher salt

1/2 teaspoon granulated sugar

Chopped green onion (white and green parts), for garnish

shrimp and bacon in a bowl and then arrange them in one layer on a disposable aluminum pan that will fit on the indirect (no fire) side of your grill. Place the tomatoes in a disposable aluminum pan that will fit on the direct (hot) side of the grill. Brush the tomatoes with olive oil.

Place the pan of shrimp and bacon on the indirect side and the pan of tomatoes on the direct side. Close the lid and grill for 5 minutes. Open the lid. If the tomatoes have softened and are a little charry, remove them from the grill. Close the lid and grill for 2 to 3 minutes longer, or until the shrimp are just turning pink, firm, and cooked through.

Put the tomatoes in a blender or food processor and add the vinegar, salt, and sugar. Process to a smooth purée. Transfer the tomato purée and the grill-roasted shrimp and bacon to a large skillet and warm through. Serve over the grits, garnished with chopped green onion.

BIG BOWL OF MUSSELS
with GRILLED POTATO DIPPERS

Mussels, clams, and other closed-shell shellfish need high heat before they'll open. At the same time, you don't want the shells to burn. So, arrange them on a perforated grill rack or a grill griddle that has been preheated on the grill, close the lid, and grill just until the shells open. Don't peek too much, or you'll let the heat escape and the shellfish will take longer to cook. Instead of soaking up the winey liquid with bread, add even more flavor with Grilled Potato Dippers.

Serves 4

GRILLED POTATO DIPPERS

4 medium baking potatoes, peeled, each cut into 8 spears

¼ cup (60 ml) olive oil

2 garlic cloves, minced

1 tablespoon finely chopped fresh flat-leaf parsley

Kosher salt and freshly ground black pepper

MUSSELS

2 pounds (1 kg) mussels in the shell (or clams)

⅓ cup (80 ml) olive oil

4 garlic cloves, minced

⅔ cup (160 ml) dry white wine

½ cup (21 g) finely chopped mixed fresh herbs, such as tarragon, basil, chives, and flat-leaf parsley

Prepare a hot fire in your grill. Heat a perforated grill rack or a grill griddle over the grill fire.

For the Grilled Potato Dippers, toss the potatoes with the olive oil, garlic, and parsley on a baking sheet or in a disposable aluminum pan. Season with salt and pepper and set aside.

Scrub the mussels well under cold running water, pulling off their stringy beards. Discard any mussels that are not tightly closed.

Heat the olive oil in a saucepan over medium heat and sauté the garlic until golden, about 3 minutes. Stir in the wine and herbs. Remove from the heat and set aside.

Arrange the potato wedges on the perforated grill rack or griddle and grill, gently turning every 2 minutes or so, until the potatoes have good grill marks and are tender, about 12 to 15 minutes. Transfer the potatoes to a serving bowl and arrange the mussels on the grill rack or griddle. Close the lid and grill for 4 to 5 minutes, or until the shells have opened. Immediately spoon about 1 teaspoon of the garlic, herb, and wine mixture into each opened mussel. Discard any mussels that have not opened.

To serve, arrange the mussels in individual pasta bowls or a large shallow serving bowl and pour the remaining garlic, herb, and wine mixture over them. Soak up all that goodness with the potato dippers.

SHORE DINNER *on the* GRILL

A breeze blows in from the ocean at sunset, while a driftwood fire blazes on the sandy beach. A grill rack awaits fresh lobster, ears of corn, and new potatoes. Sliced tomatoes and a pan of brownies complete the meal. That's a shore dinner you can have anywhere, with a little imagination. Place the grilled lobsters, corn, and potato skewers in the middle of a newspaper-covered table. Everyone can help themselves. No plates necessary. Make your excursion easier by having the fishmonger cut the lobsters in half lengthwise and remove the veins and sacks from the heads.

Serves 8

2 pounds (1 kg) new potatoes

8 (1¼- to 1½-pound/567 to 680 g) Maine lobsters, halved lenthwise and cleaned

3 sticks (340 g) unsalted butter, melted, divided

Kosher salt and freshly ground black pepper

8 ears fresh corn, unshucked

2 tablespoons finely snipped fresh chives

Soak 8 wooden skewers in water for 30 minutes.

Par-cook the potatoes, in batches, for 5 minutes on high in the microwave. Thread the par-cooked potatoes on the pre-soaked skewers.

Keep the lobsters on ice or refrigerated until grilling. Prepare a hot fire in your grill.

Reserve 2 sticks (227 g) of the butter for serving with the lobster. Brush the potato skewers with some of the remaining melted butter and season with salt and pepper.

Oil a perforated grill rack and place it on the grill. Grill the potato skewers, turning every minute, until they have good grill marks and the potatoes are tender when tested with a fork, about 5 minutes. Grill the corn in the husk, turning every minute, for 5 minutes. Pull the husks back from the corn—the silks will come right off. Take thin pieces of husk and wrap them around each of the pulled back husks to make natural handles for the corn. Place the potato skewers and the corn on a large platter, drizzle with the remaining butter used for brushing, and sprinkle with chives.

Place the lobsters, cut-side down, on the grill rack and grill for 6 to 8 minutes. Turn the lobsters over and cook until the flesh is firm and white, another 6 to 8 minutes. To serve, give everyone 2 grilled lobster halves, a potato skewer, and an ear of corn. Pass the remaining melted butter.

PLANKED SALMON *with* SMOKY ORANGE AIOLI *and* SALSA VERDE

Planking is the easiest way to grill salmon (see How to Plank, page 19). We like to use thick cedar oven planks on the grill, but you can also use thinner grilling planks—just make sure you soak them in water first so they don't burn up on the grill. Make sure your salmon fillet fits the plank you have (trim the fish, if necessary). The combination of wild-caught pink salmon, fragrant orange aioli, and green herbs both looks and tastes great. The plank is also your serving platter.

Serves 4

SMOKY ORANGE AIOLI

1 cup (227 g) mayonnaise

2 garlic cloves, minced

1 teaspoon freshly grated orange zest

Juice of 1 orange

1 teaspoon smoked paprika

SALSA VERDE

1 bunch fresh flat-leaf parsley

3 garlic cloves, minced

2 tablespoons capers

1 teaspoon freshly grated lemon zest

1 cup (240 ml) olive oil

Kosher salt

PLANKED SALMON

1 (1½-pound/680 g) salmon fillet, skin removed

Soak a cedar grilling or oven plank in water for at least 1 hour.

Prepare a medium-hot indirect fire in your grill, with the fire on one side and no fire on the other for plank grilling (see How to Plank, page 19).

For the Smoky Orange Aioli, combine all the ingredients in a bowl.

For the Salsa Verde, cut the stems off the parsley and place the parsley, garlic, capers, lemon zest, and olive oil in a food processor or high-speed blender and process until puréed. Season with salt and set aside.

Trim the salmon fillet to fit the plank, if necessary. Place the salmon on the plank; spread the aioli over the salmon and top with the Salsa Verde. Place the plank on the grill grate on the indirect side. Close the grill lid and cook until the fish begins to flake when tested with a fork in the thickest part, 20 to 30 minutes.

Serve the salmon on the plank.

WHITEFISH *with* HORSERADISH SAUCE *and a* KISS OF SMOKE

The Great Lakes are still teeming with whitefish. If you live or vacation in a harbor town, you'll likely see a commercial smokehouse or encounter do-it-yourselfers who fashion a smoker out of an old refrigerator. At home, you can grill-smoke fish in about 60 to 90 minutes, depending on how thick the fillets are. Since you're not cold-smoking whitefish to save for the winter, you don't need to brine them first. Simply brush the fillets with apple cider, season, and then put them on the indirect side of the grill when the wood begins to smolder (maple, hickory, or oak would be a good choice). The fish will take on a bronze color and be moist, tender, and aromatic with smoke. Pair them with two other Midwestern favorites: horseradish and sour cream. Leftover fish and sauce can make a dandy dip to serve with veggies or crackers.

Serves 4

HORSERADISH SAUCE

¾ cup (170 g) sour cream

3 tablespoons (41 g) prepared horseradish

WHITEFISH

4 cups (1 L) apple cider, divided

8 whitefish fillets

1 tablespoon lemon pepper

1 tablespoon white pepper

Chopped fresh flat-leaf parsley, for garnish

For the Horseradish Sauce, combine the sour cream and horseradish in a bowl. Cover and refrigerate until ready to serve.

Prepare a medium-hot indirect fire in your grill or smoker with a kiss of smoke (see page 17), preferably using maple, hickory, or oak.

Fill a doubled-up disposable aluminum pan with 3½ cups (840 ml) of the apple cider and place it on the hot side of the grill.

Brush the fillets with the remaining ½ cup (120 ml) of apple cider and sprinkle with the lemon and white peppers. Set the fish in a separate disposable aluminum pan.

When you see the first wisp of smoke from the wood, place the pan of fish on the indirect side of the grill, close the grill lid, and smoke until the fish fillets are opaque and begin to flake when tested with a fork, about 1 hour.

Arrange the fish on a platter and place a dollop of horseradish sauce and a sprinkling of parsley atop each fillet.

CAST-IRON SCALLOPS *with* BROWNED LEMON BUTTER *and* CHIVES

When Judith lived in Vermont, a food-truck fishmonger would drive into Burlington once a week with fresh-caught haddock and, sometimes, scallops from Maine. Atlantic scallops grow wild in the waters from Maine to the Outer Banks of North Carolina. In Maine, the scallop season runs from December through April; in North Carolina, it's later January through early April. The most eco-friendly scallops are labeled as "dayboat," "dive," or "diver," which indicates by-hand harvest with a rake or tongs, or by scuba diving. To expertly grill these beauties, heat a cast-iron skillet on the grill until really, really hot and then sear them. The butter browns quickly in the pan. The only other embellishment is a squeeze of lemon juice and a sprinkle of chives.

Serves 2

12 ounces (340 g) dry-pack
    sea scallops

Olive oil, for brushing

2 tablespoons unsalted butter

Finely chopped fresh chives,
    for garnish

1 lemon, quartered, for serving

Prepare a hot fire in your grill. Place a large cast-iron skillet on the grill grates, close the lid, and let the skillet heat until the inside bottom starts to look gray, at least 15 minutes.

Pat the scallops dry with paper towels.

Brush one side of the scallops with olive oil and place them oiled-side down, in the hot skillet. Sear for 1½ to 2 minutes, or until well browned. Add the butter to the pan and grill the scallops on the other side for about 1 minute.

Serve the scallops in a shallow serving bowl, browned-side up, with the browned butter, a sprinkle of chives, and a squeeze of lemon juice.

OAK-GRILLED TROUT
with CAMPFIRE POTATOES

Fly fishing—the elegant arc of a line being cast, the art of making the perfect fly or lure—is meditative, a thinking-person's fishing. Maybe that's why this activity figures in Richard Brautigan's novel Trout Fishing in America *or the film* A River Runs Through It. *Wearing hip boots or waders or sitting in a canoe, the fisherman casts off in a cold, spring-fed stream and hopes for the best. Many trout-fishing locales have a catch-and-release rule, but there are still places where you can keep the trout you reel in. In this recipe, whole, dressed trout are stuffed with butter, lemon, and herbs and grilled over aromatic wood, like oak. Packet potatoes—thinly sliced potatoes drizzled with olive oil, seasoned to taste, and enclosed in a foil packet—are the classic campfire accompaniment.*

Serves 4

CAMPFIRE POTATOES

Olive oil

4 medium baking potatoes, peeled and thinly sliced

1 small white onion, thinly sliced

Kosher salt and freshly ground black pepper

OAK-GRILLED TROUT

4 (12-ounce/340 g) dressed trout, heads and tails on

½ cup (113 g) unsalted butter, melted

2 lemons, thinly sliced

1 cup (42 g) chopped mixed fresh herbs, such as basil, parsley, dill, and chives

Chive blossoms on stems, for garnish

For the Campfire Potatoes, lay two 18 x 18-inch (46 x 46 cm) sheets of heavy-duty aluminum foil on a flat surface and brush with olive oil. Equally divide and layer the potato and onion slices on the 2 foil sheets. Season with salt and pepper and drizzle with a little olive oil. Wrap and seal the foil to form 2 packets.

Prepare a wood fire in your grill (see page 16), preferably with oak.

For the trout, brush the inside cavities with some of the butter, place 3 lemon slices in each cavity, and sprinkle a quarter of the mixed herbs over the lemon slices in each. Brush the outsides of the trout with any remaining butter. Place the fish in 2 oiled, hinged metal fish baskets or on an oiled, perforated grill rack. When you see the first wisp of smoke from the wood, place the fish and the potato packets on the grill and close the lid. Grill for 5 minutes, then turn the fish and potatoes, close the lid, and grill for another 5 minutes. Keep cooking and turning until the fish is opaque and just beginning to flake when tested with a fork, and the potatoes are tender, about 15 to 20 more minutes.

To serve, place the potatoes on the outer edge of a platter. Set the trout in the middle. Garnish with the chive blossoms.

GRILLED MAHI-MAHI
with MACADAMIA BUTTER

Also known as dolphinfish or dorado, mahi-mahi (which means "very strong" in Hawaiian) is a sweet, white-fleshed fish from both Atlantic and Pacific waters. The Monterey Bay Aquarium rates this as a "Best Choice" for sustainability and environmental reasons. We like it because it keeps its shape and texture on the grill. With a flavored butter enriched with macadamia nuts, also from Hawaii, you get a memorable dish that tastes more complicated than it is to make. For a contrast, serve this with fresh sliced papaya with a squeeze of lime juice, a little chopped cilantro, and a sprinkling of red pepper flakes. Or choose any other flavored butter from the Butter-Up Chart on page 161.

Serves 4

MACADAMIA BUTTER

½ cup (113 g) unsalted butter, at room temperature

¼ cup (50 g) chopped macadamia nuts

¼ cup (21 g) chopped fresh flat-leaf parsley

1 tablespoon freshly squeezed lemon juice

GRILLED MAHI-MAHI

4 (6-ounce/170 g) skinless mahi-mahi fillets

Olive oil, for brushing

Kosher salt and freshly ground black pepper

For the Macadamia Butter, combine all the ingredients in a small bowl. Set aside.

Prepare a hot fire in your grill.

Rinse the fish and pat it dry with paper towels. Brush the fish with olive oil and season with salt and pepper.

Brush the grill grates with olive oil.

Place the fish on the grill. Grill for 10 minutes per inch (2.5 cm) of thickness, turning once, until the fish is firm.

Serve the mahi-mahi on a platter and add a dollop of Macadamia Butter on top of each fillet.

→ FISH SUBSTITUTIONS ←

Additional fish names are included here to aid you in your fish shopping, so that it is easy to substitute fish depending on what looks fresh and is available. Delicate-textured fish are more difficult to grill directly over the grill grates. Use a grill rack, disposable aluminum pan(s), or heavy-duty foil packets for these tender fish.

TEXTURE	MILD FLAVOR	MODERATE FLAVOR	FULL FLAVOR

FIRM	Barramundi
	Blackfish
	Halibut
	John Dory
	  (St. Peter's Fish)
	Lobster
	Monkfish
	Oreo Dory
	Prawns
	Red Drum (Redfish)
	Sea Bass (Loup de Mer)
	Shrimp
	Soft-Shell Crab
		Clams
		Cobia (Sergeant Fish)
		Drum (White Sea Bass)
		Moonfish (Opah)
		Salmon
		Shark
		Skate
		Striped Marlin
		  (Nairagi)
		Sturgeon
		Swordfish
		Yellowfin Tuna
			Cuttlefish
			Escolar
			Marlin (A'u)
			Mussels
			Octopus
			Oysters
			Squid
			Triggerfish

MODERATELY FIRM	Catfish Grouper Ocean Perch (Redfish) Orange Roughy Pompano Sea Scallops Snapper Striped Bass Walleye Whitefish	Arctic Char Barracuda Bonito Mahi-Mahi (Dorado) Sablefish (Black Cod) Sea Bream (Daurade) Sea Trout (Weakfish) Tilapia Trout	Amberjack Kingfish King Mackerel Mackerel Mullet Permit Wahoo (Ono) Yellowtail Jack (Hamachi) Yellowtail Snapper

DELICATE	Bass (freshwater)
	Cod
	Crappie (freshwater)
	Flounder
	Hake (Whiting)
	Pink Snapper
	  (Opakapaka)
		Herring
		Pomfret (Butterfish,
		  Dollarfish)
		Shad
		Smelt (Whitebait)
			Anchovy
			Bluefish
			Buffalo Fish
			Sardine

MESQUITE-SMOKED BISON CHILI

Native, hardy, and grass-fed, American bison are making a comeback with those who put a premium on natural and local foods. Buffalo used to roam as far east as West Virginia, but now they are predominantly ranched in the Dakotas, Colorado, Kansas, Oklahoma, and Texas. Lean and flavorful, bison meat makes a mean chili. And when you simmer it on the grill with mesquite smoke (or oak or pecan), you'll feel like you're in a Larry McMurtry novel, hanging out around the campfire with the Lonesome Dove cowboys.

Serves 8

- 1 pound (454 g) ground bison or buffalo
- 2 teaspoons ground cumin
- 1 garlic clove, minced
- 1 medium yellow onion, finely chopped
- 1 Anaheim chile, stemmed, seeded, and finely chopped
- 1 poblano chile, stemmed, seeded, and finely chopped
- 2 tablespoons chili powder
- 1 (10-ounce/283 g) can diced tomatoes with green chiles
- 1 (28-ounce/794 g) can diced fire-roasted tomatoes, undrained
- 1 (15.5-ounce/440 g) can chili beans, undrained
- 1 (15.5-ounce/440 g) can kidney beans, drained and rinsed
- Kosher salt and freshly ground black pepper
- Shredded Cheddar cheese, for serving
- Sour cream, for serving
- Sliced ripe avocado, for serving
- Finely chopped tomato, for serving
- Chopped green onion (white and green parts), for serving

Prepare an indirect fire in your grill or smoker with a kiss of smoke (see page 17), using mesquite, oak, or pecan wood.

Place a large Dutch oven on the direct (hot) side of the grill. When the fire is hot, brown the bison with the cumin, garlic, and onion in the Dutch oven. Add the chopped chiles and chili powder and stir to blend. Add the diced tomatoes with green chiles, fire-roasted tomatoes, chili beans, and kidney beans. Season with salt and pepper and stir to blend. Transfer to the indirect (no heat) side of the grill.

When you see the first wisp of smoke, close the grill lid.

Grill with the lid closed, stirring every 30 minutes, for 2 hours, or until the chili ingredients and seasonings have had time to thoroughly blend.

To serve, ladle the chili into bowls and top with your favorite garnishes.

SIRLOIN *with*
WILD MUSHROOM GRILLING PASTE

Every once in a while, the Food Network airs the "Grill Girls" segment we filmed in Kansas City, and you can see us grill this steak (the video is also on YouTube, "BBQ Queens Karen Adler & Judith Fertig"). When you pair grass-fed beef from the cattle country of the Great Plains with wild mushrooms from the Pacific Northwest, you get a really beefy, "umami" flavor, making Choice beef taste like Prime. You can slather this mushroom paste on 30 minutes before grilling, but for an even deeper flavor, give it an hour or two to permeate the meat. Another serving option is to slice the meat and place it on top of slices of grilled country bread. The juices of the steak will soak into the bread, and it will be delicious—especially if you top the steak with arugula and shavings of a hard cheese like Grana Padano or Parmesan.

Serves 4 or more

- ¼ cup (7 g) dried porcini or morel mushrooms
- 2 tablespoons granulated sugar
- 1 tablespoon kosher salt
- 5 large garlic cloves, minced
- 1 tablespoon red pepper flakes
- 1 tablespoon freshly ground black pepper
- ¼ cup (60 ml) olive oil
- 4 (8-ounce/227 g) boneless sirloin steaks, 3/4 to 1 inch (1.9 to 2.5 cm) thick, from grass-fed beef if possible

Grind the dried mushrooms to a powder in a coffee or spice grinder. Transfer to a bowl and add the sugar, salt, garlic, pepper flakes, pepper, and olive oil. Stir until fully combined and the mixture forms a paste.

Slather the steaks on both sides with the porcini paste. Cover and refrigerate for at least 30 minutes.

Prepare a hot fire in your grill. Grill the steaks for 3 to 4 minutes on each side for medium-rare. Let the steaks rest for about 5 minutes, covered with foil, before slicing or serving.

Serve the steaks whole on a platter or slice each steak into ¾-inch- (1.9 cm-) thick slices and then platter the meat. Slicing the steak is a great way to stretch it to serve 6, and maybe even 8, diners.

CAST-IRON COWBOY STEAK
with BACON BOURBON BUTTER

The secret to a great steakhouse steak is consistent high heat. You can get that outdoors by heating up a cast-iron griddle on the grill until very, very hot. This method will deliver a delicious charry crust on your steak, only made better by a finishing pat of Bacon Bourbon Butter. Make the flavored butter early in the day to let the flavors blend, then keep it chilled. Instead of a cast-iron grill griddle, you could also use two large cast-iron skillets. We recommend grapeseed oil because it has a higher smoke point for cooking the steaks over high heat.

Serves 4

BACON BOURBON BUTTER

4 ounces (113 g) unsalted butter, at room temperature

1 shallot, finely minced

2 slices bacon, cooked until crisp and finely crumbled

1 tablespoon bourbon or whiskey

1 teaspoon Worcestershire sauce

1 tablespoon finely chopped fresh flat-leaf parsley

Kosher salt and freshly ground black pepper

COWBOY STEAK

4 cowboy steaks, bone-in rib-eye steaks, or boneless rib-eyes, about 1½ inches (3.8 cm) thick

Olive or grapeseed oil, for brushing

Kosher salt and freshly ground black pepper

Finely chopped fresh flat-leaf parsley, for garnish

For the Bacon Bourbon Butter, mash the butter with the shallot, crumbled bacon, bourbon, Worcestershire, and parsley. Season with salt and pepper. Form into a cylinder on a sheet of plastic wrap or waxed paper and chill for several hours, or until firm.

Prepare a hot fire in your grill. Place a cast-iron grill griddle on the grill grates, close the lid, and let it heat for at least 20 minutes. When the griddle starts to have a grayish appearance, it's hot enough to grill.

Brush the steaks with oil and season both sides with salt and pepper.

Grill the steaks for 2 to 3 minutes on each side for medium-rare. The steaks will smoke heavily, but will produce a blackened, charred exterior and a pink, juicy interior.

Let the steaks rest off the grill, covered with foil, for 5 minutes.

Serve the steaks on a platter, place a pat of Bacon Bourbon Butter on each steak, and sprinkle with parsley.

CREOLE COFFEE-RUBBED
BEEF TENDERLOIN

When you want to do it up big for a special occasion, this recipe is perfect. You can serve the beef tenderloin right off the grill or grill it earlier in the day and serve it chilled. You can hardly have too much beef tenderloin because it makes a great steak-and-eggs combo or sandwich the next day. Another tip: Buy a whole beef tenderloin and trim it up yourself to save money. Simply trim away any fat or silver skin and tie the narrow end under the roast so that the whole tenderloin is the same thickness and grills evenly. Or, you can trim off the narrow end and grill that separately as a snack for the barbecuer! This dish has the flavor of a New Orleans party—and they know how to celebrate!

Serves 8 to 12

CREOLE COFFEE RUB

2 tablespoons very finely ground chicory coffee, Kona coffee, or espresso

1 tablespoon Spanish paprika

1 tablespoon lightly packed dark brown sugar

1 teaspoon dry mustard

2 teaspoons kosher salt

1 teaspoon freshly ground black pepper

1 teaspoon freshly ground white pepper

1 teaspoon dried tarragon

1 teaspoon dried oregano

2 teaspoons cayenne pepper

CREOLE SAUCE

1 cup (227 g) mayonnaise

2 tablespoons prepared horseradish

2 tablespoons Creole or whole-grain mustard

For the Creole Coffee Rub, combine all the ingredients in a bowl and blend well. Keep in a sealable jar on your kitchen counter until ready to use.

For the Creole Sauce, stir the mayonnaise, horseradish, mustard, lemon juice, and 2 teaspoons of the Creole Coffee Rub together until well blended. Season with salt and pepper. Cover and refrigerate until ready to serve.

Prepare a hot fire in your grill.

For the tenderloin, fold the tapered end under the meat, then tie the tenderloin at intervals with kitchen twine so the tenderloin becomes a cylinder and will grill evenly. Brush the tenderloin with olive oil and sprinkle all over with Creole Coffee Rub.

Grill, covered, for 10 minutes, turning a quarter turn after 5 minutes. Brush again with olive oil and grill for 10 to 12 more minutes, turning a quarter turn every 5 minutes, until a meat thermometer registers 130°F (54.5°C) for rare, or to your desired doneness.

Let the tenderloin rest for 5 minutes and then remove the twine.

2 teaspoons freshly
  squeezed lemon juice
2 teaspoons Creole Coffee
  Rub (see page 120)
Kosher salt and freshly
  ground black pepper

TENDERLOIN
1 (6- to 8-pound/2.7 to 3.6 kg)
  beef tenderloin, trimmed
Olive oil, for brushing
Creole Coffee Rub (see page
  120), for sprinkling
4 cups (170 g) baby arugula

To serve, line a platter with the arugula. Slice the tenderloin and serve it on the bed of arugula, accompanied by Creole Sauce.

TEXAS-STYLE BRISKET *in a* BAG

A few years ago, we did cooking classes throughout Texas. While we were driving to each city, we stopped at barbecue joints. Every place we went seemed to use a different type of oak—blackjack, red heart, white, and post oak. "Different oaks for different folks" was our bad joke. But it makes perfect sense that barbecuers use the local wood that is readily available. As Kansas City barbecue aficionados, we hate to admit that Texas barbecuers really have a way with beef, from clod (shoulder) at Kreuz Market in Lockhart to brisket at Franklin Barbecue in Austin. Aaron Franklin has made his brisket famous. Franklin says that rub-wise, "The way we roll here in central Texas is half salt and half pepper." He recommends a "packer" cut, which means the whole brisket, in Cryovac, not just the pointed end or flat. This is a labor of barbecue love, so figure on about 12 hours, start to finish. Here, you'll need oak in 20-inch (50 cm) "logs" or smaller wood chunks. Your brisket will be "done" way before it is tender. Cherry Chipotle Barbecue Sauce (page 128) is mighty fine with this brisket.

Serves 12 or more

SALT 'N' PEPPER RUB
¼ cup (68 g) kosher salt
¼ cup (28 g) freshly ground
   black pepper

BRISKET
2 cups (480 ml) apple juice
10 to 12 pounds (4.5 to 5.5 kg)
   beef brisket, including the full
   flat and the point section, well
   marbled, at room temperature
Two paper grocery sacks
Favorite barbecue sauce, for
   serving

For the Salt 'n' Pepper Rub, mix the salt and pepper together and set aside. Pour the apple juice into a spray bottle.

For the brisket, trim off all but about ¼ to ½ inch (6 mm to 1.3 cm) of fat with a boning or other slim, sharp knife and discard. If you like, leave the deckle (the thicker, pointy, fattier end) on the meat for Kansas City–style burnt ends. Trim off any membrane or silver skin. Pat dry with a paper towel. Spray the meat with apple juice. Season the meat with the Salt 'n' Pepper Rub and evenly and gently pat it all over.

Prepare an indirect fire in your smoker using oak in 20-inch (50 cm) "logs" or smaller wood chunks (see How to Slow Smoke, page 17). Place a disposable aluminum pan filled with water in the smoker, either next to or under where the brisket will cook, depending on your equipment. The smoker will be ready when the temperature reads about 225°F (107°C).

Place the brisket on the cool side of the smoker, fat-side up, with the fatty end closest to the fire, and close the lid. Cook for 6 hours, adding wood as needed to keep the fire going. Use an instant-read thermometer to check temperature. Remove the brisket from the smoker when its temperature reaches 165°F (74°C). Spray the brisket with apple juice. Insert one end of the brisket into a paper grocery sack, and then slide the other end in a second paper grocery sack, so the brisket is double-bagged from each end. Return to the smoker for 2 hours or so, or until the internal temperature reaches 205°F (96°C). Remove the brisket from the smoker. Remove the bags and spray one more time with apple juice and let rest on a cutting board for 15 minutes. Trim off the burnt ends and serve separately. To serve, slice the brisket against the grain into ¼-inch- (6.4 mm-) thick pieces and arrange on a platter along with your favorite BBQ sauce.

ROOT BEER RIBS

The classic flavors in American root beer—anise, vanilla, sugar, spice—just naturally go well with pork. So, it's not too much of a stretch to use a root beer marinade and a rub with root beer flavors for ribs, and then finish with a root beer glaze. Five-spice powder is available at better grocery stores, Asian markets, or online at Penzeys or other spice emporia. We recommend removing the membrane from the back of the ribs so that the aromatic rub and glaze can penetrate the meat more. Use needle-nose pliers to remove the membrane from the just-out-of-the-refrigerator slab of ribs. If the ribs are room temperature, it is more difficult to remove the membrane because it will break apart. For the wood, choose apple, cherry, pecan, or oak (or a combination).

Serves 8

RIBS

2 (1- to 1½-pound/450 to 675 g) slabs baby back ribs

3 (12-ounce/355 ml) bottles root beer, divided

ROOT BEER RIB RUB

1 tablespoon five-spice powder

1 tablespoon ground coriander

¼ cup (55 g) packed dark brown sugar

2 tablespoons garlic salt

2 tablespoons sweet Hungarian paprika

2 tablespoons freshly ground black pepper

ROOT BEER GLAZE

½ cup (120 ml) clover or other amber honey

4 ounces (113 g) unsalted butter

Favorite barbecue sauce, for serving (optional)

For the ribs, remove the membrane from the back of the chilled ribs using needle-nose pliers. Place the ribs in a large disposable aluminum pan or a large roasting pan and pour in 20 ounces (591 ml) of the root beer. Place 1 bottle of the root beer in a spray bottle; reserve the remaining ½ cup (120 ml) of root beer for the glaze.

Cover and let the ribs marinate in the refrigerator for at least 4 hours or overnight, turning once.

Prepare an indirect fire in your grill or smoker to slow smoke (see page 17), using apple, cherry, pecan, or oak wood (or a combination).

For the Root Beer Rib Rub, combine all the ingredients in a large glass jar with a tight-fitting lid. Secure the lid and shake to blend. This rub will keep in the kitchen cupboard for several months.

Drain the ribs and pat them dry with a paper towel. Transfer the ribs to a large baking sheet. Sprinkle the rub all over the ribs.

For the Root Beer Glaze, combine the remaining ½ cup (120 ml) of the root beer with the honey and butter in a saucepan over medium-high heat. Stir to combine, and cook until just bubbling, then transfer to a bowl.

When you see the first wisp of smoke, place the ribs on the smoker rack. Cover and slow smoke at 250°F (121°C) for 2 hours, spraying with root beer every 30 minutes. When the rib meat has pulled back from the bones, carefully turn the ribs over. Brush them with the glaze. Close the lid and keep slow smoking for 30 more minutes. Turn the ribs again and brush again with the glaze. Close the lid and slow smoke for 15 more minutes so that the ribs develop a beautiful sheen.

To serve, leave as whole slabs on a platter or cut into individual ribs. Pass your favorite barbecue sauce, if you like, or the remaining Root Beer Glaze.

⟶ FOAM ON THE RANGE ⟵

Starting off as a popular drugstore soda fountain drink in the late 1800s, root beer production surged after Prohibition began in 1920. Today, there are over 2,000 brands. Like a good barbecue spice rub, root beer can have a lot of flavor components: vanilla, birch, licorice root, wintergreen, sarsaparilla root, nutmeg, anise, molasses, cinnamon, clove, and honey. Just as a cold root beer and a hot dog go together, so do root beer and pork ribs. Look for one that is sweetened with cane sugar or honey for the best flavor.

Barq's, Atlanta, Georgia—strong root beer flavors

Berghoff Famous Old-Fashioned Root Beer, Chicago, Illinois—smooth and crisp, with notes of birch

Boylan's, Haledon, New Jersey—hints of wintergreen and anise

IBC, St. Louis, Missouri—smooth, anise and molasses flavors, with a bit of a bite

Stewart's, Denver, Colorado—flavored with acacia, quillaia, and yucca extracts

DOUBLE-SMOKED KENTUCKY HAM
with APRICOT BBQ SAUCE

Treat yourself to a cooked country ham from one of these Kentucky artisans: Father's Country Hams in Bremen, Broadbent's in Kuttawa, or Colonel Bill Newsom's Aged Kentucky Country Ham in Princeton. Spiral-sliced ham allows smoke to penetrate farther into the meat in a shorter amount of time, so smoking can be done in an hour or two at the most. Use apple or other fruitwood, hickory, pecan, or oak (or a combination). Don't cook it too long, or the sliced meat will dry out. If you want a mahogany-colored ham with lots of smoke, and you have some time on your hands, choose a country-cured or precooked whole ham rather than the spiral-cut. The outside "rind" on a whole ham keeps the inner meat from drying out. Score it all over with a cross-hatch pattern to help the smoke penetrate. Smoke for 2 to 6 hours, depending on the desired smokiness.

Serves 10 to 12

APRICOT BBQ SAUCE

2 cups (256 g) finely chopped dried apricots

1 cup (227 g) apricot preserves

1 cup (142 g) finely chopped yellow onion

1 cup (142 g) finely chopped red bell pepper

2 banana peppers, seeded and finely minced

3 garlic cloves, minced

1 cup (240 ml) cider vinegar

3/4 cup (160 g) lightly packed dark brown sugar

1 tablespoon ground chipotle pepper

2 teaspoons kosher salt

1 teaspoon ground cumin

1/2 teaspoon ground ginger

HAM

1 (5- to 7-pound/2.27 to 3.17 kg) cooked spiral-sliced ham

For the Apricot BBQ Sauce, in a large saucepan, combine all the ingredients and cook over medium-high heat for about 25 minutes, stirring frequently, until the sauce thickens. Set aside. The BBQ sauce will make about 5 cups (1.2 L) and will keep in an airtight container in the refrigerator for several weeks.

Prepare an indirect fire in your grill with a kiss of smoke (see page 17), using apple or other fruitwood, hickory, pecan, or oak (or a combination).

Place the ham in a doubled-up disposable aluminum pan and place the pan on the indirect side of the grill. Close the lid and smoke for 30 minutes. Baste with the Apricot BBQ Sauce and pan juices, close the lid, and smoke for 30 minutes. Repeat the basting and smoke for 30 minutes more, or until the ham is bronzed and reaches the desired smokiness. You'll need to taste it to determine the level of smokiness.

Serve the smoked ham on a large platter with additional Apricot BBQ Sauce on the side. The ham can be cooked a day or two ahead, refrigerated, and then warmed up in a 350°F (177°C) oven.

CHERRY CHIPOTLE PORK BUTT

Pork shoulder—cut and packaged as pork butt, Boston butt, or pork blade roast—is one of the easiest and most satisfying foods to slow smoke. With a little chipotle in the rub, some cherry wood (or apple, hickory, or a combination) in the smoker, and a finishing touch of Cherry Chipotle Barbecue Sauce, this dish is a blue ribbon winner. On a recent Fourth of July with rainy weather, Judith set up her electric bullet smoker in the garage and left the doors open to smoke the pork for 4 hours the evening before, then finished it overnight in the oven. An hour at 350°F (177 °C) at the front or back end of cooking ensures a good bark, that dark outer crust. Easy! If you're going to slow smoke something for a long time, why not do more than you need and freeze the rest? That's the way. The sauce is adapted from one by the greats, the late Karen Putman, Flower of the Flames, who won every major barbecue competition.

Serves 12

CHIPOTLE RUB

¹⁄₂ cup (56 g) freshly ground black pepper

¹⁄₂ cup (56 g) sweet Hungarian paprika

3 tablespoons (21 g) ground chipotle pepper

¹⁄₄ cup (28 g) garlic powder

¹⁄₄ cup (68 g) onion salt

3 tablespoons (21 g) dry mustard

3 tablespoons (21 g) celery seeds

CHERRY CHIPOTLE BARBECUE SAUCE

2 cups (454 g) ketchup

1 cup (227 g) sour cherry preserves

¹⁄₂ cup (120 ml) sour cherry juice (bottled)

¹⁄₂ cup (110 g) packed dark brown sugar

For the Chipotle Rub, combine all the ingredients in a large glass jar with a tight-fitting lid. Secure the lid and shake to blend. This rub will keep in the kitchen cupboard for several months.

For the Cherry Chipotle Barbecue Sauce, whisk all the ingredients together in a medium saucepan over medium heat. Bring to a simmer and cook for 10 to 15 minutes, or until the flavors have blended. Let cool. You should have about 4 cups (946 ml). Use right away or transfer to a glass bottle or jar and secure the lid. Store in the refrigerator for several months.

For the pork butt, use a small, sharp knife to trim excess fat from the pork, leaving about ½ inch (1.3 cm). Pat the rub all over the pork butts. Place the pork in a doubled-up disposable aluminum pan. Let rest for 30 minutes. Place the cherry juice in a spray bottle.

Prepare an indirect fire in your grill or smoker to slow smoke (see page 17), using cherry, apple, or hickory wood, or a combination.

When you see the first wisp of smoke, place the pan of pork butts on the smoker rack and close the lid.

3 tablespoons (44 ml)
cider vinegar

1 tablespoon Worcestershire
sauce

1 garlic clove, minced

1 teaspoon onion powder

2 tablespoons bottled chipotle
sauce, or 1 teaspoon ground
chipotle pepper

PORK BUTT

2 (3½-pound/1.6 kg) boneless
pork butts

2 cups (480 ml) bottled
cherry juice

Slow smoke at 250°F (121°C) for 4 hours, spraying with cherry juice every hour after the second hour. Keep slow smoking for 4 more hours, spraying with cherry juice every hour, until the pork reaches 165°F (74°C). Insert a fork into the pork and twist to check for tenderness. If the meat shreds easily, it is tender and done. If it is not tender, continue to slow cook for another hour, or until it is fork-tender. Alternatively, after the initial 4 hours on the smoker, spray the pork butts with cherry juice, cover the pan tightly with foil, and place in a 250°F (121°C) oven to slow cook for at least 4 hours, or even slow cook overnight in the oven at 225°F (107°C) for 8 hours.

When ready to serve, pull the meat apart while it is still warm, discarding the fat, and arrange the shredded meat on a platter. Serve with Cherry Chipotle Barbecue Sauce on the side.

SESAME-SOY MARINATED PORK TENDERLOIN *with* SMOKED APPLESAUCE

Because we live in a barbecue capital—Kansas City—and all the accoutrements are readily available, we are always experimenting with smoke flavors. Recently, we took a stab at smoking apples. It's a natural with grilled pork tenderloin. While the pork is marinating, smoke the apples (using apple, hickory, oak, or pecan wood) and make the fresh applesauce, which is so good you might not look at regular applesauce the same way ever again. But don't feel like you need to fire up the smoker just for apples: when you're already smoking something else, why not put a pan or two of apple quarters on to smoke? The Smoked Applesauce will keep in the refrigerator for several weeks or in the freezer for several months.

Serves 8

SMOKED APPLESAUCE

8 tart apples, such as Granny Smith, Lodi, or Transparent, peeled, cored, and quartered

1 cup (240 ml) clover or other amber honey

1 teaspoon freshly squeezed lemon juice

¼ teaspoon kosher salt

SESAME-MARINATED PORK TENDERLOIN

4 (12-ounce/340 g) pork tenderloins

1 cup (240 ml) soy sauce

⅓ cup (80 ml) toasted sesame oil

1 tablespoon freshly grated ginger

3 garlic cloves, minced

Prepare an indirect fire in your grill or smoker with a kiss of smoke (see page 17).

For the Smoked Applesauce, place the apple quarters in a doubled-up disposable aluminum pan. When you see the first wisp of smoke, place the pan on the indirect side. Cover and smoke for 1 hour, or until the apples have a smoky aroma and a burnished appearance. Transfer the apples to a medium saucepan over medium-high heat. Stir in the honey. Reduce the heat and simmer for 15 to 20 minutes, or until the apples are soft. Mash the apples in the pan until chunky and then stir in the lemon juice and salt. Makes 2 cups (480 ml), which can be refrigerated for several weeks or frozen for several months.

For the pork tenderloin, place the pork in a large resealable plastic bag. Add the soy sauce, sesame oil, ginger, and garlic to the bag and shake a bit to disperse. Marinate in the refrigerator for at least 2 hours or overnight.

Prepare a hot fire in your grill.

Remove the pork from the marinade and discard the bag and marinade. Grill the pork for 5 minutes per side, turning a quarter turn at a time until the internal temperature registers 140 to 145°F (60 to 63°C).

Slice the grilled pork into 1-inch- (2.5 cm-) thick slices. Serve with the Smoked Applesauce on the side.

PLANKED CHICKEN BREASTS
with CHILE LIME SOFRITO

Over years of giving cooking classes, we have met students from all kinds of culinary traditions. Those who grew up in Puerto Rico are partial to a flavoring paste known as sofrito, the slowly simmered and caramelized vegetable flavoring paste that goes into arroz con pollo. A batch of sofrito takes a little longer than an hour to cook, but like caramelized onions, it's so worth it. So, go slow and let your kitchen fill with its fabulous aroma. Then use some of your sofrito to flavor this dish (and freeze the rest). This sofrito recipe is adapted from one by Annie Pettry, chef at Decca in Louisville, Kentucky.

Serves 4

CHILE LIME SOFRITO

3 tablespoons (42 g) unsalted butter

4 yellow onions, chopped

2 jalapeno peppers, stemmed, seeded, and minced

1 teaspoon kosher salt, plus more to taste

1 garlic clove, minced

¼ cup (20 g) finely chopped fresh cilantro

Grated zest and juice of 1 lime

PLANKED CHICKEN BREASTS

4 (5¼-ounce/150 g) boneless skinless chicken breasts

For the Chile Lime Sofrito, melt the butter over medium heat. Add the onions and peppers and salt and reduce the heat to medium-low. Cook the onions slowly, stirring often, until they are soft and light golden, 1 hour. Add the garlic and cook until soft, 8 to 10 minutes. Remove from the heat and add the cilantro, lime zest, and lime juice. Taste and adjust the seasoning with salt. Let cool. Use right away or refrigerate up to 1 week.

Soak 2 cedar grilling planks in water for an hour. Prepare an indirect fire in your grill with a fire on one side and no fire on the other (see How to Plank, page 19).

Place the chicken breasts on the planks and spread with half of the Chile Lime Sofrito.

Place the planks on the indirect (no-heat) side of the grill. Close the lid and cook for 30 minutes, or until a meat thermometer inserted in the thickest part of a breast registers 160°F (71°C). Serve the chicken on the planks with the additional sofrito on the side. The additional sofrito may also be refrigerated to use later in the week.

PIQUILLO PEPPER–STUFFED CHICKEN *with* GREEN OLIVE TAPENADE

Piquillo peppers, descendants of Peru's chile de arbol, require a long, hot, dry growing sea-son, which fits Sonoma's Dry Creek Valley to a T. Gardeners and farmers get their piquillo pepper seeds from the Chile Pepper Institute at New Mexico State University or online from Peppermania. Piquillos are not edible raw; instead, they're smoke-roasted over wood and then packed in brine in jars or cans. If you grow piquillos, simply smoke-roast them until they're done (see How to Smoke-Roast Vegetables, page 167). Banana peppers are a good substitute for the piquillo peppers, too.

Serves 8

GREEN OLIVE TAPENADE

1 cup (227 g) pimento-stuffed green olives, roughly chopped

¹/₂ cup (42 g) chopped fresh flat-leaf parsley

1 tablespoon capers

PIQUILLO PEPPER–STUFFED CHICKEN

8 (5¹/₄-ounce/150 g) boneless skinless chicken breasts

8 ounces (227 g) fresh goat cheese, Boursin, or cream cheese, at room temperature

8 jarred piquillo peppers or 8 jarred roasted red peppers (about 16 ounces/454 g)

Kosher salt and freshly ground black pepper

Olive oil, for brushing

Prepare a medium-hot fire in your grill.

For the Green Olive Tapenade, combine all the ingredients in a bowl.

Place each chicken breast between waxed or parch-ment paper and flatten with a meat mallet to an even ¹/₂-inch (1.3 cm) thickness. With a knife or a rubber spatula, spread 1 ounce (28 g) of goat cheese down the center of each chicken breast, then top with 1 piquillo pepper, opened and spread out. Season with salt and pepper. Start from a long edge of the chicken and roll up. Secure with toothpicks. Brush with olive oil.

Grill the chicken for 4 to 5 minutes per quarter turn, 16 to 20 minutes total.

To serve, remove the toothpicks and cut the chicken into 1-inch (2.5 cm) slices, then arrange them on a platter. Dollop the grilled chicken slices with tapenade and serve.

SIZZLING WINGS *with*
HOT SAGE BUTTER *and* ROMANO

Drizzled with Hot Sage Butter and sprinkled with a Wisconsin-made Romano just as the chicken comes off the grill, this is our version of finger-lickin' good. Just make sure you have enough napkins. Leaving the chicken wings whole is the simplest and fastest way to prepare them.

Serves 4

2 pounds (1 kg) chicken wings, drumsticks, or thighs

1 (12-ounce/340 ml) bottle Italian-style vinaigrette

Grated zest and juice of 1 lemon

4 ounces (113g) unsalted butter

4 to 6 fresh sage leaves

½ teaspoon red pepper flakes

2 ounces (50 g) freshly grated Romano cheese

Rinse the chicken under cold running water and pat it dry. Place the chicken in a large resealable plastic bag.

Pour the vinaigrette into a medium bowl and add the lemon juice and zest. Reserve half of the lemon-flavored vinaigrette and pour the rest over the chicken. Seal the bag and mix by turning it several times. Marinate the chicken in the refrigerator for at least 20 minutes or up to 2 hours.

In a small saucepan over medium heat, melt the butter with the sage leaves and pepper flakes. Lower the heat and cook until the butter browns and is infused with the sage flavor, about 15 to 20 minutes. Remove from the heat.

Prepare a medium-hot fire in your grill.

Remove the chicken from the bag and discard the bag and marinade. Pat the chicken dry and place the chicken directly over the fire. Use the reserved lemon-vinaigrette marinade to baste the chicken every 5 minutes for the first 15 minutes. Continue to grill, turning every 5 minutes, until the chicken pieces are nicely browned and crisp all over and the meat begins to shrink at the base of the bone. Total cooking time is about 20 minutes for wings and 30 minutes for thighs or drumsticks.

To serve, arrange the chicken on a platter. Reheat the Sage Butter: it should be hot enough that when you pour the hot butter over the hot wings, it actually sizzles. Pour the Hot Sage Butter over the chicken and sprinkle with Romano.

GRILLED CHICKEN SPIEDINI
with FRESH BASIL CREAM SAUCE

Karen's friend Lee Hitchler shared this recipe from her son Spencer Lomax, who is a chef. His secret for the spiedini is to use chicken tenders, not whole chicken breasts. We suggest fusilli pasta for this dish, but any other pasta that will hold the sauce, like fettuccine or penne, would work well, too.

Serves 6

FRESH BASIL CREAM SAUCE

1 quart (846 ml) half-and-half

Juice of 1 lemon

¼ cup (21 g) chopped fresh basil

1 teaspoon kosher salt

½ cup grated Parmesan cheese

GRILLED CHICKEN SPIEDINI

1 pound (454 g) fusilli pasta

3 pounds (1.4 kg) chicken tenders

Olive oil

1 cup (42 g) breadcrumbs

1 cup (113 g) freshly grated Parmesan cheese

Grated zest of half a lemon

1 pint (310 g) cherry tomatoes, halved

1 (5-ounce/142 g) package baby arugula

½ cup (56 g) freshly grated Parmesan cheese, for garnish

¼ cup (21 g) chopped fresh basil, for garnish

For the Fresh Basil Cream Sauce, heat the half-and-half in a large saucepan (large enough to hold the finished pasta) over medium-high heat. Stir until it is reduced by a third. Add the lemon juice, basil, salt, and Parmesan. (The sauce may curdle just a bit.) Set aside and keep warm.

Cook the pasta according to the package directions, and drain it, reserving about a cup of pasta cooking water.

Prepare a medium-hot fire in your grill. Soak 10 or 12 thick wooden skewers in water for 30 minutes.

Cut the chicken tenders in halves or thirds so that you have fairly even chunks of chicken. Skewer 4 or 5 pieces of chicken onto each wooden skewer, keeping a tiny bit of space between each chicken piece. Lay the skewers on a baking sheet. Drizzle with olive oil.

Combine the breadcrumbs, Parmesan, and lemon zest and spread onto a separate baking sheet. Roll the skewered chicken in the crumb mixture until evenly coated.

Brush the grill grates with oil. Grill the chicken skewers for about 8 to 10 minutes, turning once, until they reach your desired doneness.

To assemble the dish, spoon the hot pasta into the saucepan with the cream sauce. Reheat over low heat until the pasta and sauce are warm, adding a splash of pasta water if necessary to thin the sauce. Remove the chicken from the skewers and place atop the pasta. Add the cherry tomatoes and arugula. Toss to combine. Garnish with chopped basil and grated Parmesan.

CORN HUSK–WRAPPED TURKEY BREAST *with* HATCH CHILES *and* MONTEREY JACK

When both New Mexico Hatch chiles and fresh corn come into season in summer, make this recipe, which will forever banish the notion that turkey is only for Thanksgiving. Because the turkey is skinless, it needs to be covered. We wrap it in green corn husks (and then grill the corn). Hatch chiles need to be roasted or grilled first, and we can buy them that way in Kansas City at places like Whole Foods Market. You can also grill fresh Hatch chiles whole, then stem and seed them to use in this recipe, or buy roasted Hatch chiles in cans. The corn husks give a slightly sweet flavor to the turkey, which nicely balances the tang and heat of the chiles. Use piñon, fruitwood, corn cobs, grapevines, pecan, oak, or maple wood.

Serves 4 to 6

2 (3-pound/1.4 kg) boneless skinless turkey breast halves

4 roasted Hatch chiles, stemmed and seeded

8 ounces (227 g) sliced Monterey Jack cheese

1 tablespoon olive oil

16 long, fresh, green corn husks from 4 to 6 ears of corn

Prepare an indirect fire in your grill or smoker with a kiss of smoke (see page 17), using piñon, fruitwood, corn cobs, grapevines, pecan, oak, or maple wood.

Rinse the turkey under cold, running water and pat it dry. Make a lengthwise pocket slit in each turkey breast and stuff each with half of the Hatch chiles and Monterey Jack. Lightly brush with the olive oil. Wrap each breast with 8 green corn husks, tied or toothpicked in place. You want the turkey breast to be covered but not too tightly. Place the turkey on the smoker rack. When you see the first wisp of smoke, cover and smoke at 250°F (121°C) until an instant-read meat thermometer inserted in the thickest part of a breast registers 160 to 165°F (71 to 74°C), 1½ to 2 hours. The turkey will have a hint of pink. Remove it from the smoker and let it rest for about 10 minutes.

To serve, remove the corn husks from the turkey breasts. Slice into ½-inch- (1.3 cm-) thick slices and place on a platter.

CHAPTER 5

Vegetables

TERROIR, THE MICROCLIMATE SO IMPORTANT IN WINE, ALSO comes through in vegetables. Silver Queen corn thrives in the reliably moist summers east of the Mississippi River, while Peaches 'n' Cream toughs out the dry spells farther west. Festivals around the country celebrate the bounty of the region, from the Midwest Morel Fest in Ottawa, Illinois to the Chile Pepper Festival in Phoenix, Arizona, the Gilroy Garlic Festival in California, and the Official Circleville Pumpkin Show in Ohio.

Everyone knows that a tomato picked fresh from your own backyard tastes the best, but every region has its favorite: Jersey tomatoes have a sweet-tart tang that is the flavor of summer for East Coasters. But don't brag to northwest Ohioans. Tomatoes grown in the rich farmland of the former Great Black Swamp are prized for their flavor—so much so that Heinz bottles their famous tomato ketchup in Fremont, Ohio. Dry-farmed Kurlbaum's Heirloom Tomatoes reach peak juiciness in Kansas City, Kansas.

Gardeners from Montana to Maine love the hardiness of winter squash, while gardeners in the sultrier states watch as their zucchini grow from finger to foot size in 24 hours.

For spring grillers we have an exquisite platter of Purple, Green, and White Asparagus with Grilled Lemon Butter (page 142), and for summer try the Planked Beefsteak Tomatoes with Goat Cheese (page 152) and the Grilled Corn with Confetti Pepper Butter (page 158), plus a dozen more flavored butters from our Butter-Up Chart (see page 161) to slather on your hot-off-the-grill vegetables. In the autumn and winter try these tasty dishes for the grill and smoker: Ember-Roasted Brussels Sprouts with Browned Butter Vinaigrette (page 146) and Barbecuer's White Bean Casserole (page 143). We even have your holiday side dishes for the grill, which by the way, save you much-needed space in your indoor oven. For Thanksgiving or Christmas or New Year's, try the Smoked Acorn Squash with Brown Sugar Butter (page 164), Grilled Artisan Bread and Italian Sausage Stuffing (page 165), Smoke-Roasted Root Vegetables with Garlic and Thyme (page 166), and Grilled Butternut Squash with Garlic and Olives (page 156).

For every season, every occasion, every barbecuer, there's a delicious vegetable just waiting its turn on the grill.

Grilled Avocados, Tomatoes, and Lemons

Purple, Green, and White Asparagus
with Grilled Lemon Butter

Barbecuer's White Bean Casserole

Ruby Slipper Beets

Ember-Roasted Brussels Sprouts
with Browned Butter Vinaigrette

All-Year-Round Fire-Roasted Vegetables

Baby Vegetables and Microgreens
with Charry Lime Vinaigrette

Grilled Green Tomatoes with
Mississippi Comeback Sauce

Planked Beefsteak Tomatoes with Goat Cheese

Grilled Tomatoes on the Vine with Smoky Garlic Aioli

Grilled Butternut Squash with Garlic and Olives

Ember-Roasted Eggplant
with Garlic, Lemon, and Olive Oil

Grilled Corn with Confetti Pepper Butter

Chars and Stripes Vegetable Platter

Smoked Acorn Squash with Brown Sugar Butter

Grilled Artisan Bread and Italian Sausage Stuffing

Smoke-Roasted Root Vegetables with Garlic and Thyme

GRILLED AVOCADOS, TOMATOES, and LEMONS

Grill-warmed avocados, tomatoes, and lemons make a simply delicious vegetable platter. Just that little time on the grill—enough to scorch and get grill marks—makes a big taste difference. If you like, accompany this with grill-warmed corn tortillas. Make sure to use ripe or almost-ripe avocados and tomatoes; overly ripe fruits will get mushy when cooked.

Serves 6 to 8

4 ripe avocados, halved and pitted with the skin on

3 lemons, halved

3 large ripe tomatoes, sliced ³/₄ inch (1.9 cm) thick

1 small red onion, thinly sliced

Olive oil, for brushing

Chopped fresh cilantro, for garnish

Coarse kosher salt and freshly ground black pepper

Prepare a hot fire in your grill.

Lightly brush the cut sides of the avocados and lemons and one side of the tomato slices with olive oil. Place the avocado halves directly over the fire, skin-side down, and grill for 1 minute, just to warm them. Set avocados aside to cool. Grill the tomato slices directly over the fire, oiled-side down for about 2 minutes. Set on a platter, some positioned grilled-side up.

Grill the lemon halves for about 1 to 2 minutes on the cut sides only. Let cool.

Slip the skins off the cooled avocados, cut each half into quarters, and place them on top of the tomatoes. Squeeze the avocado with a grilled lemon half. Scatter the onion slices and sprinkle with cilantro. Season with salt and pepper.

To serve, squeeze with more lemon and set the remaining grilled lemon halves on the platter as garnish.

PURPLE, GREEN, *and* WHITE ASPARAGUS *with* GRILLED LEMON BUTTER

When asparagus is in season, look for fresh, thick spears that will take well to grill-roasting —a deliciously easy way to grill asparagus. In addition to the green varieties, look for Purple Passion or Queen Victoria purple asparagus and the French-favorite, white, which farmer Lee Jones of The Chef's Garden, a 300-acre vegetable garden in Huron, Ohio, is making chic on this side of the Atlantic. No matter which color asparagus you grill-roast, fresh asparagus is so beautiful and so delicious on its own that you don't want anything to hide its color or overpower its flavor. We think a Grilled Lemon Butter is just the ticket. Use a butter made from grass-fed cows for the best flavor.

Serves 4

ASPARAGUS

6 ounces (170 g) thick spears green asparagus

6 ounces (170 g) thick spears purple asparagus

6 ounces (170 g) thick spears white asparagus

Olive oil, for brushing

Kosher salt and freshly ground black pepper

GRILLED LEMON BUTTER

4 ounces (113 g) unsalted butter

1 lemon, halved

Kosher salt

1 tablespoon finely snipped fresh chives

Prepare an indirect fire in your grill and place a perforated grill rack on the no-heat side.

Snap the tough ends of the asparagus off one at a time, at the place where the spear naturally bends and breaks, and discard the ends. Arrange the spears on a baking sheet, brush with olive oil, and season with salt and pepper.

Transfer the asparagus to the grill rack, close the lid, and grill-roast the asparagus for 15 to 20 minutes, turning occasionally, or until the asparagus is blistered and crisp-tender.

For the Grilled Lemon Butter, place the butter in a pan to melt on the hot side of the grill. At the same time, grill the lemon halves, cut-side down, for 1 to 2 minutes, or until they have good grill marks. Squeeze the grilled lemon into the melted butter, season with salt, and stir in the chives.

To serve, arrange the colorful asparagus spears on a platter and drizzle with the Grilled Lemon Butter.

BARBECUER'S WHITE BEAN CASSEROLE

Today's high-style barbecuers, like the restaurant Q39 in Kansas City, add smoked sausage to this dish and place it on the smoker for a hearty, succulent finish. Shovel a path out to your grill or smoker in the winter to make this dish—it's that good.

Serves 8

1 pound (454 g) dry white navy beans

1 tablespoon unsalted butter

1 medium yellow onion, diced

2 to 3 garlic cloves, minced

¼ cup (30 g) all-purpose flour

2 cups (480 ml) chicken stock

5 ounces (142 g) smoked sausage, sliced about ¼ inch (6.4 mm) thick

1 teaspoon kosher salt

¼ teaspoon freshly ground black pepper

1 (14-ounce/397 g) can diced fire-roasted tomatoes

¾ teaspoon fresh thyme leaves

Soak the beans for 8 hours or overnight in a bowl with enough water to cover.

Drain off the water from the beans. Transfer them to a large saucepan and add more water to cover. Bring the beans to a boil over medium-high heat, then reduce the heat and simmer, covered, for 1½ hours, or until tender.

Prepare a hot indirect fire with a kiss of smoke (see page 17) in your grill with apple or oak wood.

When the beans are tender, drain off the water and set the beans aside. In a small saucepan over medium-high heat, melt the butter and sauté the onion until transparent, about 4 minutes. Stir in the garlic and cook for 1 minute. Add the flour and whisk together to make a roux. Whisk in the chicken stock until smooth. Pour the mixture into the beans and stir in the smoked sausage, salt, pepper, tomatoes, and thyme. Transfer the bean-sausage mixture to a doubled-up disposable aluminum pan.

When you see the first wisp of smoke on the grill, place the pan on the indirect (no-heat) side. Close the lid and smoke for 1 hour at 325°F (163°C), or until the casserole has a good smoky aroma.

RUBY SLIPPER BEETS

How about a recipe that can transform an everyday root vegetable into a dazzler—like Dorothy's ruby slippers in The Wizard of Oz? Arrange these grilled beet slices on a white or pale blue platter, then dollop with goat cheese, scatter with fresh raspberries, and drizzle with Fresh Raspberry Sauce for a glistening, scrumptious showstopper. The Fresh Raspberry Sauce would also be good drizzled over grilled peaches and topped with a scoop of ice cream or over Somewhere over the Rainbow Ice Cream Cake (page 184).

Serves 4

FRESH RASPBERRY SAUCE

12 ounces (340 g) fresh raspberries

⅓ cup (150 g) granulated sugar

¼ cup (60 ml) water

RUBY SLIPPER BEETS

8 unpeeled medium beets

Olive oil, for brushing

Garlic powder

Freshly ground black pepper

6 ounces (170 g) fresh raspberries, for garnish

4 ounces (225 g) fresh goat cheese

Microgreens, pea shoots, or fresh thyme sprigs, for garnish

For the Fresh Raspberry Sauce, stir the raspberries, sugar, and water together in a medium saucepan over medium-high heat. Bring to a boil, then reduce the heat and simmer for 15 minutes, stirring occasionally, until the sugar has dissolved and the berries have cooked down to a pulp. Remove from the heat. Pour the mixture through a sieve placed over a 4-cup (1 L) glass measuring cup. Use a wooden spoon to stir the raspberry pulp in the sieve so that it drips down into the measuring cup: you should have about 1 cup (240 ml). Discard the remaining berry pulp in the sieve. Let the syrup cool and then pour it into a glass jar. Cover and chill until ready to use. Fresh Raspberry Sauce can be made up to a week in advance.

Scrub the beets and trim the tops and root ends. Slice the beets ½ inch (1.3 cm) thick. Brush them with olive oil on both sides and season with garlic powder and pepper.

Prepare a medium-hot fire in your grill. Grill the beets, turning occasionally, until they start to bend when touched with grill tongs and are crisp-tender, about 25 minutes.

To serve, arrange the grilled beets on a platter. Scatter with the raspberries. Dollop the beets with goat cheese and drizzle with Fresh Raspberry Sauce and garnish with microgreens.

EMBER-ROASTED BRUSSELS SPROUTS *with* BROWNED BUTTER VINAIGRETTE

Roasted Brussels sprouts are delicious, but ember-roasting sprouts on the grill takes them to a whole new level. Instead of the mushy kind boiled to oblivion or the indoor-roasted kind, which take up valuable oven space during the holidays, try these on your grill. This recipe is inspired by David Falk of Boca in Cincinnati (who makes Brussels sprouts that people fight over) and Bryce Gilmore in Austin, a Food & Wine Best New Chef in 2011. The Marcona almonds in the vinaigrette add to the roasty-toasty flavor.

Serves 4

**EMBER-ROASTED
BRUSSELS SPROUTS**

2 large stalks Brussels sprouts

Olive oil, for brushing

Kosher salt and freshly ground
 black pepper

**BROWNED BUTTER
VINAIGRETTE**

4 ounces (113 g) unsalted butter

¹/₄ cup (60 ml) sherry vinegar

2 tablespoons water

¹/₄ cup (43 g) Marcona almonds

Kosher salt and finely ground
 black pepper

Prepare a hot indirect fire in your grill.

For the Brussels sprouts, depending on the size of the stalk and your grill surface, create a tray from double-layered heavy-duty aluminum foil or use a doubled-up disposable aluminum pan. Place the stalks of sprouts on the foil or in the pan, brush them all over with olive oil, and season with salt and pepper.

Place the tray next to the embers or on the grill grate next to the fire. Close the lid and grill for 15 minutes, then carefully lift and turn the pan 180 degrees with long-handled grill tongs so the sprouts scorch on the other side. Baste the sprouts again with olive oil. Close the lid and turn and baste every 15 minutes, or until the sprouts are tender when pierced with a fork, about 45 minutes total.

For the Browned Butter Vinaigrette, melt the butter in small skillet over medium heat and cook, stirring occasionally, for 5 minutes, or until the butter is browning and has a nutty aroma. (Don't let it get dark brown.) Remove from the heat immediately. Transfer to a food processor or blender and add the vinegar, water, and almonds. Purée until smooth. Season with salt and pepper.

To serve, transfer the whole stalk of sprouts to a rustic serving platter or snip off the sprouts and place on the platter. Spoon the Browned Butter Vinaigrette over all.

ALL-YEAR-ROUND FIRE-ROASTED VEGETABLES

When vegetables get a drizzle of olive oil, a sprinkle of salt and pepper, and then the heat of live fire for caramelization—it's close to savory perfection. Year-round vegetables include beets, bok choy, broccoli, cabbage, carrots, cauliflower, chard, endive, fennel, garlic, kale, lettuce, mushrooms, green onions, leeks, shallots, potatoes, and turnips. Whether you buy them at the farm stand or grocery store, or grow them in your own backyard, these stalwarts from the vegetable world have a bonus of being very affordable. How to grill? You need a hot fire and your choice of colorful vegetables to make a sensational platter of veggies that have great grill marks and are crisp or tender: your choice.

Serves 8

GARLIC BREADCRUMBS

½ loaf stale bakery bread, roughly chopped

¼ cup (60 ml) olive oil

4 garlic cloves, thinly sliced

FIRE-ROASTED VEGETABLES

4 baby bok choy, halved lengthwise

24 green onions, trimmed

4 carrots, peeled and halved lengthwise

1 red onion, trimmed and cut into ½-inch (1.3 cm) slices

2 sweet onions, trimmed and cut into ½-inch (1.3 cm) slices

4 portobello mushrooms

2 fennel bulbs, quartered lengthwise

1 head cauliflower, cut into ½-inch (1.3 cm) slices

2 turnips, cut into ½-inch (1.3 cm) slices

Olive oil, for brushing

Kosher salt and freshly ground black pepper

For the Garlic Breadcrumbs, pulse the bread in the food processor until fine crumbs are formed. In a large skillet heat the olive oil over medium-high heat. Add the breadcrumbs when the oil is hot and toss and cook until the crumbs are toasted. Add the garlic and toss with the hot crumbs, then transfer to a bowl and set aside. You should have about 3 cups (187 g). Crumbs can be made ahead and stored in a resealable bag in the refrigerator for several days or in the freezer for several months.

Prepare a hot fire in your grill.

Rinse and pat the vegetables dry. Brush the vegetables with olive oil and season with salt and pepper.

Arrange the bok choy (cut-side down), green onions, and carrots perpendicular to the grill grates. Add the onion slices and grill for about 3 to 5 minutes, or until they have good grill marks. Transfer them to a platter.

Grill the portobello mushrooms for 6 to 8 minutes, cap-side down, or until they have good grill marks and are soft. Set aside. Grill the fennel, cauliflower, and turnips for 3 to 5 minutes per side, on all sides, or until charred with good grill marks. Arrange on the platter and top all the vegetables with the Garlic Breadcrumbs.

BABY VEGETABLES *and* MICROGREENS *with* CHARRY LIME VINAIGRETTE

We know the Charry Lemon Vinaigrette (page 86) is similar to this lime version, but it's so good it bears repeating, with the tweak of substituting lime for the lemon and adding cilantro. Tender baby vegetables just take a short blast of fire in this recipe, so they're still crisp and delicious but with the flavor of the grill. All of that is enhanced by the caramelized lime dressing and the crisp microgreens. This almost looks too pretty to eat. Almost.

Serves 4

BABY VEGETABLES AND MICROGREENS

4 ounces (113 g) baby radishes

4 ounces (113 g) baby carrots, with some of the green tops

4 ounces (113 g) baby leeks, trimmed

4 ounces (113 g) baby yellow patty pan squash

Olive oil, for brushing

Kosher salt and freshly ground black pepper

2 ounces (57 g) microgreens

CHARRY LIME VINAIGRETTE

2 limes

1 tablespoon seasoned rice wine vinegar

1 tablespoon chopped fresh cilantro

1 teaspoon Dijon mustard

1 teaspoon sorghum or maple syrup

¼ cup (60 ml) olive oil

Kosher salt and freshly ground black pepper

Prepare a medium-hot fire in your grill.

Brush the radishes, carrots, leeks, and squash with olive oil and season with salt and pepper. Place in a grilling basket or on a perforated grill rack. Grill for 4 to 5 minutes, turning often, until the vegetables have just started to brown at the edges.

For the Charry Lime Vinaigrette, zest the limes and set the zest aside. Halve the limes and grill them, cut-side down, for 1 to 2 minutes, or until they have good grill marks. Squeeze the juice of the grilled lime halves into a bowl. Add the lime zest, vinegar, cilantro, mustard, sorghum, and olive oil and whisk together until well blended. Season with salt and pepper.

Arrange the vegetables on salad plates and garnish with microgreens. Spoon the vinaigrette over all and serve.

HOOPING IT UP WITH BABY VEGETABLES

Hoop houses, also known as high tunnels, are greenhouses made of PVC pipe and plastic sheeting. Made from kits or from materials gathered at a home store, these tunnels extend the growing season earlier in the spring and later in the fall. They reflect the "can-do" spirit of innovative farmers all over the country.

Baby vegetables especially love the more nurturing environment of a hoop house, protected from weather extremes. Goetz Farm in Riga, Michigan, grows winter greens and baby carrots in high tunnels, despite a foot of snow on the ground in February. Next Step Produce, an organic farm in Charles County, Virginia, specializes in high-maintenance baby ginger. Poplin Farms in Albemarle, North Carolina, put in hoop houses after the frigid winter of 2010; now they grow Fairy Tale eggplant and heirloom tomatoes in more-controlled conditions. Creative Growers Farm in Noti, Oregon, grows baby fennel as well as baby carrots.

But whether you have a hoop house or protected garden spot, you can still grow baby vegetables. Some baby vegetables are simply immature versions of the fully ripened variety, and others are miniature. Picked smaller, they often have a sweeter, more delicate flavor than larger varieties. Here are some to try in your own garden:

Baby leeks—pick young
Baby carrots—pick young
Baby Table Queen green and gold and crook squash—miniature, but pick young
Baby yellow or green patty pan summer squash—miniature, but pick young
Baby zucchini—pick young
Fairy Tale or Calliope eggplant—miniature
French green beans—pick young
Hakurei turnips—pick young
Lunchbox peppers—miniature
Radishes—pick young

GRILLED GREEN TOMATOES
with MISSISSIPPI COMEBACK SAUCE

Remoulade combined with Thousand Island dressing equals Mississippi Comeback Sauce: THE *sauce of the South. It's a condiment to spread on sandwiches and burgers, a dipping sauce for raw and grilled vegetables, and a salad dressing to boot. Try it with grilled foods like chicken, fish, and seafood, and in this recipe with grilled green tomatoes. Make this sauce a day ahead so the flavors can blend for optimum taste. For a different presentation, overlap each grilled green tomato with an uncooked slice of fresh red tomato. If you have yellow tomatoes, include them on the platter for a trio of colors. Garnish with red and yellow grape or cherry tomatoes. Top with thin slices of red onion, if you like, and a sprinkling of snipped chives and sprigs of basil and parsley.*

Serves 6 to 8

MISSISSIPPI COMEBACK SAUCE

1 cup (227 g) mayonnaise

¼ cup (60 ml) olive oil

¼ cup (60 ml) ketchup

¼ cup (60 ml) chili sauce

Grated zest and juice of 1 lemon

1 garlic clove, minced

1 tablespoon freshly grated onion

1 teaspoon Dijon mustard

2 teaspoons Worcestershire sauce

½ teaspoon freshly ground black pepper

½ teaspoon hot sauce

GRILLED GREEN TOMATOES

3 to 4 large green tomatoes, sliced ¾-inch (1.9 cm) thick

Olive oil, for brushing

2 teaspoons seasoning salt or kosher salt

For the Mississippi Comeback Sauce, combine all the ingredients in a bowl. Cover and refrigerate overnight or for up to 1 week.

Prepare a medium-hot fire in your grill.

Brush the tomato slices with olive oil and sprinkle with the salt.

Grill the tomato slices for about 3 minutes, turn, and grill the other side for another 3 minutes, or until you have good grill marks.

Arrange the grilled tomato slices on a platter and place a bowl of the sauce in the center of the platter, or spoon the sauce over the tomatoes.

PLANKED BEEFSTEAK TOMATOES *with* GOAT CHEESE

Planking vegetables is so very easy because you usually aren't cooking the vegetables, merely heating them through and letting them sit on the warmed plank to pick up a bit of the woody flavor of the plank.

Serves 6 to 8

2 to 3 large tomatoes, like beef-steak, sliced medium thick

Kosher salt and freshly ground black pepper

Olive oil

4 ounces (113 g) fresh goat cheese

1/2 cup (20 g) chopped fresh herbs, such as chives, oregano, parsley, or basil

Balsamic vinegar, for drizzling

Soak 1 or 2 grilling planks (cedar, maple, or oak) in water for 1 hour. Prepare a medium-hot indirect fire in your grill for planking (see page 19).

Set the tomato slices on the planks. Season the tomatoes lightly with salt and pepper and drizzle with olive oil. Crumble the goat cheese on top of each tomato slice.

Set the planks on the indirect side of the grill and close the lid. Plank for about 15 minutes, or until the tomatoes are warmed through and the cheese is soft.

Serve on the planks for an interesting presentation with a sprinkle of fresh herbs and a drizzle of balsamic vinegar.

GRILLED TOMATOES ON THE VINE
with SMOKY GARLIC AIOLI

You can buy tomatoes on the vine at the grocery store or snip them from your own garden. Grilled on the vine, tomatoes take on a rustic, garden-to-grill quality that makes you look at—and taste—them in a new way. If you like to grow your own tomatoes, plant cluster tomatoes or cherry or grape tomatoes to replicate this recipe. Like pizza and tacos, aioli has crossed over from exotic to mainstream. If you smoke garlic ahead of time, you'll be a step ahead in making the aioli. If not, you can just add a judicious dash of bottled liquid smoke.

Serves 6 to 8

SMOKY GARLIC AIOLI

2 large eggs

1 tablespoon freshly squeezed lemon juice

1 tablespoon Dijon mustard

2 to 4 garlic cloves, smoke roasted (see page 167), or 2 to 4 fresh garlic cloves, minced, plus ½ teaspoon bottled liquid smoke flavoring

1½ cups (375 ml) olive oil

GRILLED TOMATOES

2 clusters of tomatoes on the vine (about 2 pounds/1 kg)

Olive oil, for brushing

Fresh basil sprigs, for garnish

For the Smoky Garlic Aioli, combine the eggs, lemon juice, mustard, and garlic (and liquid smoke, if using) in a food processor or blender. Pulse to blend and then, with the motor running, very slowly add the olive oil until thick and creamy. Transfer to a bowl and chill until ready to serve. You should have about 2 cups (500 ml). Leftover aioli keeps refrigerated in an airtight container for up to 3 days.

Prepare a medium-hot fire in your grill.

Rinse and pat dry the tomatoes, keeping them on the vine. Brush them with olive oil and place on the grill, vine-side up so the vine is away from the heat. Let them char for 1 to 2 minutes, then change the position to get charring on the sides. Do not let the tomatoes get mushy by overcooking them.

Remove from the fire with a spatula so that the tomatoes do not fall off the vine.

To serve, arrange the vines on a platter and scatter with basil sprigs. Set the bowl of aioli on the platter and pass.

GRILLED BUTTERNUT SQUASH
with GARLIC *and* OLIVES

We made a French heirloom pumpkin version of this recipe in BBQ Bistro and loved it so much; we knew we had to give it another life in this book. In this case, we grill-roast the sliced squash in an aluminum pan. You want a butternut or Hubbard squash, several small acorn squashes, or a small, tender pumpkin like a sugar or pie pumpkin that you can buy before Halloween and keep in a cold place until Thanksgiving. You can simply cut the squash into rings; for pumpkin, it's easier to cut it into wedges to grill. The squash or pumpkin will be velvety, aromatic, and so unbelievably delicious that you will start to crave it, as we have. This vegan, gluten-free side dish is also great for those with dietary restrictions.

Serves 4 to 6

¹⁄₄ cup (60 ml) olive oil

3 large garlic cloves, sliced

1 medium-size butternut or
Hubbard squash, stemmed,
seeded, peeled, and cut into
2-inch (5 cm) slices or wedges

20 black, dry-cured olives,
pitted and halved

1 teaspoon chopped fresh
thyme, or ¹⁄₂ teaspoon
dried thyme

Kosher salt and freshly
ground black pepper

Prepare a medium-hot indirect fire in your grill.

In a saucepan over medium heat, warm the oil and garlic together until the garlic is fragrant, about 4 minutes.

Arrange the squash slices, olives, and thyme in two sets of doubled-up disposable aluminum pans. Drizzle with the olive oil-garlic mixture and then season with salt and pepper.

Place on the indirect (no-heat) side of the grill, close the lid, and grill for 20 minutes. Open the lid and turn the squash slices over. Close the lid and grill for 15 to 20 minutes more, or until the squash is fork-tender.

To serve, transfer the squash wedges to a platter and drizzle with the juices from the pan; scatter the olives over the squash and serve warm.

EMBER-ROASTED EGGPLANT
with GARLIC, LEMON, *and* OLIVE OIL

We have had sort of a girl crush on Gabrielle Hamilton, the fiction-writing, James Beard Award–winning chef-owner of Prune in New York City's East Village. We read her cookbook in our culinary book group. We watched her PBS outing on The Mind of a Chef. And then we actually had dinner at Prune. She had us at eggplant, which she cooks whole, directly over the flame of the restaurant's gas range. We translate that to the grill, which gives an even deeper smoky flavor. Scooped from its blackened skin, the eggplant is delicious served at room temperature in individual bowls with a slice of grilled bread to scoop it all up.

Serves 4

1 (1- to 1¹/₂-pound/450 to 680 g) purple eggplant

4 to 8 slices artisan bread, brushed with olive oil

1 garlic clove

1 teaspoon coarse kosher salt

1 tablespoon freshly squeezed lemon juice

3 tablespoons olive oil, plus more for serving

Prepare a hot fire in your grill.

Place the whole eggplant in the embers or on the grill grate. Close the lid and grill for 15 minutes, turning with long-handled grill tongs every 2 to 3 minutes so that the eggplant blackens on all sides and becomes soft all the way through. Take care not to crack the skin. During the last minutes of ember-roasting, grill the bread for about 1 minute per side, or until it has good grill marks. Transfer the bread to a serving plate. Transfer the eggplant to a medium metal mixing bowl, cover with plastic wrap, and let the eggplant cool.

When the eggplant is cool enough to handle, carefully remove and discard the stem and skin, but keep the liquid remaining in the bowl. Strain the charry bits out of the liquid and then gently fork the roasted eggplant and the strained liquid back into the bowl.

With a mortar and pestle, mash the garlic with the salt until it makes a fine paste. Stir in the lemon juice and olive oil.

To serve, divide the eggplant among 4 bowls and drizzle with the garlic, lemon, and olive oil mixture. Pass the grilled bread and more olive oil at the table.

GRILLED CORN *with* CONFETTI PEPPER BUTTER

Grilled sweet corn is a summer staple in backyards from sea to shining sea. Whether your favorite variety is Silver Queen or Peaches 'n' Cream, you can be sure that a make-ahead confetti-colored butter will make grilled corn even better—if that's possible. If you want to keep this plant-based, use vegan "butter."

Serves 6 to 8

- 3 small confetti peppers in yellow, red, and orange
- 1 tablespoon olive oil
- 1 garlic clove, minced
- ½ cup (113 g) unsalted butter, at room temperature
- 1 tablespoon finely chopped fresh flat-leaf parsley
- ¼ teaspoon kosher salt
- 8 to 12 ears fresh sweet corn, shucked and silks removed

For the Confetti Pepper Butter, stem, seed, and finely chop the peppers. Heat the olive oil in a small saucepan and sauté the peppers and garlic together for 2 minutes, or until the peppers are just starting to soften. Remove from the heat and let cool to room temperature. In a bowl, using a fork, mash the peppers with the butter, parsley, and salt until well blended. Spoon the butter into a ramekin or bowl and cover with plastic wrap. The butter may also be rolled into a log and covered with plastic wrap. Chill completely and keep cold until ready to serve.

Prepare a medium-hot fire in your grill.

Grill the corn, turning frequently, until it has good grill marks all over, about 5 to 6 minutes.

Serve the corn on a platter or individual plates and slather with Confetti Pepper Butter.

CENTO
ROLLED FILLETS
ANCHOVIES®
WITH CAPERS IN OLIVE OIL
SALT ADDED
NET WT. 2 OZ. (55g)

IA 295 Z BEST BY 10-31-2017

⟶ BUTTER UP ⟵

A pat of butter can be a simple finishing touch to food hot off the grill. We recommend selecting butter made from the milk of grass-fed cows. Like grass-fed beef, this butter starts off with more flavor than that made from the milk of grain-fed cows (and has more omega-3 and omega-6 fatty acids, plus beta carotene and other good things). At grocery stores and natural foods stores, as well as farmers' markets, brands such as Organic Valley Pasture Butter (Wisconsin), Humboldt Creamery (California), and Kalona (Iowa) are easy to find.

When you add one or more ingredients to softened butter, you have a compound butter. Go mild by adding just a bit of additional ingredients or robust by adding ample quantities of herbs, spices, and seasonings.

Combine the additional ingredients with the soft butter until fully incorporated. Spoon the butter into a ramekin or bowl and cover with plastic wrap. The butter may also be rolled into a log and covered with plastic wrap. Refrigerated, the butter will keep for about a week. Frozen, the butter will keep for about 3 months (wrap in additional freezer paper or in a plastic freezer bag).

Toasting nuts, smoking or grilling vegetables, and grilling fruits before combining with the butter will create even bolder flavor. See our other compound butter recipes throughout the book: Spicy-Sweet Sorghum Butter (page 34), Macadamia Butter (page 115), Bacon Bourbon Butter (page 119), and Confetti Pepper Butter (page158).

Use these easy recipes as your blueprint for your own signature butter, beginning with 4 ounces (113 g) unsalted butter at room temperature.

Smoked Tomato and Basil Butter: Add 2 finely chopped smoked tomatoes, 1/4 cup (10 g) chopped fresh basil, and 1/4 teaspoon kosher salt.

Grilled Fig and Blue Cheese Butter: Add 1 finely chopped grilled fig, 2 tablespoons crumbled blue cheese, and 1/4 teaspoon kosher salt.

Anchovy Garlic Butter: Add 1 teaspoon anchovy paste, 1 minced garlic clove, 1 teaspoon snipped fresh chives, and 1/4 teaspoon kosher salt.

Cilantro Lime Butter: Add 2 tablespoons finely chopped fresh cilantro, 1 minced garlic clove, 1 teaspoon lime juice, 1 teaspoon lime zest, and 1/4 teaspoon kosher salt.

Grilled Shishito Butter: Add 1/4 cup finely chopped grilled shishito peppers, 1 minced garlic clove, and 1/4 teaspoon kosher salt.

CHARS and STRIPES VEGETABLE PLATTER

In a time of "I can't eat that," this vegetable platter is democracy at work. It welcomes all. It can be vegan, vegetarian, gluten-free. Plus, you can take this grilled vegetable platter concept through all four seasons. Grill whatever is freshest and most colorful and arrange it on a platter. Top with a flavored butter, or pass a vegetable-based sauce such as the Roasted Red Pepper Sauce, Smoky Garlic Aioli (page 155), or pesto at the table. For spring, grill par-boiled new potatoes threaded on skewers, thick asparagus spears, and baby leeks or carrots. For summer, as showcased in this recipe, grill zucchini, fresh corn, baby eggplant, and cherry tomatoes. For autumn, try carrots, sweet potatoes, and an assortment of winter squash, or prepare All-Year-Round Fire-Roasted Vegetables (page 147).

Serves 6 to 8

ROASTED RED PEPPER SAUCE

½ cup (86 g) toasted slivered almonds

2 jarred roasted red bell peppers, roughly chopped

2 garlic cloves, minced

1 slice white bread (crust removed; gluten-free, if desired), toasted and crumbled

1 tablespoon roughly chopped fresh flat-leaf parsley

½ teaspoon red pepper flakes

⅓ cup (80 ml) red wine vinegar

⅔ cup (160 ml) olive oil

Kosher salt and freshly ground black pepper

GRILLED VEGETABLES

4 small to medium-size zucchini

4 small to medium-size yellow summer squash

Soak 8 wooden skewers in water for 30 minutes.

For the Roasted Red Pepper Sauce, grind the almonds in a food processor. Add the roasted peppers, garlic, bread, parsley, and red pepper flakes. Blend until it becomes a paste. Add the vinegar and pulse to blend. With the motor running, gradually pour the olive oil through the feed tube in a steady stream until the mixture thickens like mayonnaise. Season to taste with salt and black pepper.

Prepare a medium-hot fire in your grill.

Rinse the vegetables and pat them dry. Halve the zucchini, summer squash, and eggplants lengthwise. Remove the husks and silk from the corn. Thread the cherry tomatoes onto the wooden skewers.

Brush the vegetables with olive oil and season with salt and pepper.

Arrange the halves of zucchini, summer squash, and eggplant cut-side down and perpendicular to the grill grates. Grill the zucchini and summer squash for 2 to 3 minutes on the cut side, or until they have good grill marks. Grill the eggplants for 6 to 8 minutes, cut-side

8 baby eggplants or Japanese eggplants

4 ears fresh corn

2 pints (340 g) cherry tomatoes

Olive oil, for brushing

Kosher salt and freshly ground black pepper

Chopped fresh herbs, such as basil, flat-leaf parsley, rosemary, or chives, for garnish

down, until they have good grill marks and are soft. Grill the corn for 1 to 2 minutes on all sides, or until the kernels are slightly charry. Grill the cherry tomatoes for 2 to 3 minutes per side, or just until the skins start to crack.

To serve, arrange the zucchini, summer squash, and eggplant halves in rows on a white platter. Position some of the vegetables grilled-side up and some grilled-side down for a colorful presentation. Cut planks from the corn cobs and place on the platter. Keep the cherry tomatoes on the skewers or remove them and add to the platter. Sprinkle all with chopped herbs. Pass the Roasted Red Pepper Sauce at the table.

·→ THANKSGIVING ON THE GRILL ←·

A couple of years ago we did a satellite media tour/Thanksgiving promotion for the Hearth, Patio & Barbecue Association. Using your outdoor kitchen makes perfect sense at holiday time, when indoor oven space is at a premium. Your grill or smoker can keep items warm, and you can "cook" on it, too. Round out your Thanksgiving menu with Smoke-Roasted Sweet Potatoes with Spicy-Sweet Sorghum Butter (page 34), Blistered Green Beans with Buttermilk Ranch Dressing (page 88), and Grilled Butternut Squash with Garlic and Olives (page 156). For a smaller gathering, try Grilled Kale Bundles with Warm Cranberry-Bourbon Vinaigrette (page 94). A make-ahead cold salad like Quinoa, Feta, and Farm-Stand Vegetable Salad (page 98) is a light and refreshing option for the groaning board. In addition to your family's traditional turkey recipe, you might try Corn Husk–Wrapped Turkey Breast with Hatch Chiles and Monterey Jack (page 137). The Ember-Roasted Brussels Sprouts with Browned Butter Vinaigrette (page 146) are killer. And, of course, these delicious side dishes.

SMOKED ACORN SQUASH
with BROWN SUGAR BUTTER

Wonderful any time of year, but especially appropriate for Thanksgiving dinner, this squash recipe has just the right amount of smokiness, and it frees up your oven! Any winter squash will do, too. Try smoking several varieties of squash like butternut, sugar pumpkin, spaghetti, and Sweet Dumpling (similar to an acorn with pale yellow and green stripes). Arranged on a platter, the colors say autumn: deep orange butternut, pale orange Sweet Dumpling, and very pale yellow spaghetti squash. If it's a big holiday dinner with lots of other dishes, you can easily quarter each of the squash to serve 12.

Makes 6 servings

3 acorn squash, halved and seeded

Olive oil, for brushing

6 tablespoons (84 g) unsalted butter

2 teaspoons ground cinnamon

2 tablespoons dark brown sugar

2 tablespoons maple syrup

1/2 teaspoon red pepper flakes (optional)

Kosher salt

Prepare a smoker or an indirect fire in the grill. Add 2 or 3 chunks of water-soaked wood of your choice, like apple or oak.

Brush the cut side of each squash with olive oil. Cover each squash half with foil. Poke holes in the foil to let the smoke through and put the squash, cut-side down, in a 225°F (107°C) smoker. Smoke for 2 hours, or until the squash is tender. Remove from the smoker.

Melt the butter in a saucepan and whisk in the cinnamon, brown sugar, maple syrup, and pepper flakes (if using), and season with salt to taste. To serve, spoon the spicy butter equally into each squash half and serve.

GRILLED ARTISAN BREAD
and ITALIAN SAUSAGE STUFFING

Using the grill for the stuffing gives it an extra bit of smokiness and char. If you prefer, grill slices of the bread whole and then break them up into pieces for the stuffing. Either way is great.

Serves 12

8 cups (336 g) cubed assorted artisan bread

Olive oil, for drizzling

$^1\!/_2$ cup (113 g) unsalted butter

1 cup (225 g) chopped celery, both leaves and stalks

1 medium yellow onion, chopped

1 jalapeño pepper, seeded and chopped (optional)

3 cups (720 ml) chicken stock

8 ounces (227 g) Italian sausage, spicy or mild, casings removed

1 teaspoon dried sage, marjoram, or rosemary

Kosher salt and freshly ground black pepper

2 large eggs, beaten

Prepare a medium-hot indirect fire in your grill. Place the bread in a couple of disposable aluminum pans. Drizzle lightly with olive oil. Set on the indirect side of the grill. Close the lid and toast the bread for about 12 minutes, or until light golden brown. Place the grill-toasted bread in a large bowl.

Melt the butter in a large skillet and sauté the celery, onion, and jalapeño for 5 minutes, or until soft. Add the chicken stock and heat until warm.

Pour the chicken stock mixture over the bread and mix well.

In the same skillet, brown the sausage. Add browned sausage and sage to the bread mixture and mix well. Taste and then season with salt and pepper. Add the eggs and mix well again.

Place the stuffing in a disposable aluminum pan and grill on the indirect side at 325°F (163°C) for about 45 to 50 minutes, or until the top gets golden brown. Do not cover the grill. Remove the stuffing and serve hot.

SMOKE-ROASTED ROOT VEGETABLES
with GARLIC *and* THYME

Why not experiment with this dish and expand your vegetable repertoire? Buy one of several root vegetables, peel them, and cut them into 1-inch (2.5 cm) pieces. Smoke-roast until they caramelize and have a smoky aroma (try oak or apple wood), then dress them with a little lusciousness—Smoky Garlic Aioli (page 155), perhaps? This is a dish you can make a meal out of, it's so good.

Serves 6 to 8

4 pounds (2 kg) root vegetables, such as carrots, turnips, parsnips, kohlrabi, rutabaga, celery root, Jerusalem artichokes, sweet potatoes, potatoes, yams, and onions

Olive oil, for drizzling

Coarse kosher salt and freshly ground black pepper

12 fresh thyme sprigs, plus more for garnish

1 recipe Smoky Garlic Aioli (page 155), for serving

Prepare a medium-hot indirect fire in your grill with a kiss of smoke (page 17), using oak or apple wood.

Scrub the vegetables, rinse, and pat dry. Peel the vegetables and cut into 1-inch (2.5 cm) pieces. Place the vegetables in two sets of doubled-up disposable aluminum pans. Drizzle with olive oil and season with salt and pepper. Stir the vegetables to evenly coat them with oil and seasonings and then tuck the thyme sprigs between the vegetables.

Place on the indirect (no-heat) side of the grill. Add the wood to the fire. When you see the first wisp of smoke, close the lid. Smoke for about 1 hour, or until each vegetable is fork-tender.

To serve, arrange the vegetables on a platter garnished with fresh sprigs of thyme. Serve the aioli on the side.

— HOW TO SMOKE-ROAST VEGETABLES —

While you're planking salmon, why not put some fresh vegetables on to smoke-roast, too? Smoke-roasting means indirect grilling with wood added to the fire for smoke. It's hotter than slow smoking but less hot than direct grilling. Smoke-roasted vegetables are delicious eaten right away or frozen for later use in soups and stews. They're not as smoky but cook faster and crisper than slow-smoked vegetables (see How to Slow Smoke Vegetables, Fruits, and Nuts, page 18).

To smoke-roast vegetables, prepare a hot indirect fire in your grill with a kiss of smoke (see page 17). Brush the vegetables with olive oil and season with salt and pepper. Place them right on the grill grates on the indirect (no-heat) side or place them in a disposable aluminum pan that will fit on your grill. When you see the first wisp of smoke, close the lid and let the vegetables start to get burnished, smoky, and delicious.

Here's the timetable for:

Bell peppers—Stem, seed, and cut in half. Smoke-roast for 30 minutes.

Chiles (piquillo, shishito, or banana peppers)—Use whole. Smoke-roast for 30 minutes.

Garlic—Trim ends of whole garlic bulb. Smoke-roast for 45 minutes, or until soft.

Onion (yellow, red, or white)—Cut in half. Smoke-roast for 45 to 60 minutes.

CHAPTER 6

Sweet Somethings

"LIFE IS UNCERTAIN. EAT DESSERT FIRST," QUIPPED ERNESTINE
Ulmer Frank, a little-known but much-quoted writer, who was born in Nebraska in 1892 and died in South Dakota in 1987. Whether it's chocolate or fruit, cake or ice cream, we want it all. And the outdoor kitchen delivers.

Chocolatier's Crostini (page 172) is as simple as grilled bread, good chocolate just starting to melt, and a sprinkle of coarse salt. Warm Chocolate Sauce (page 182) streams over an ice cream cake like molten lava.

Fruit—especially fruit high in natural sugars—takes well to the grill, and we make the most of it in every season. Grilled Valencia and Blood Oranges with Honey Orange Drizzle (page 174) in the winter, Grilled Pound Cake with Blueberry Carda-mom Compote (page 181) in the spring, Grilled Peaches with Toasted Almond Baste (page 177) or Stars and Stripes Grilled Banana Split (page 187) in summer, and Grilled Persimmons with Mascarpone and Spice Syrup (page 185) in the fall.

Naturally soft fruits—like bananas, apricots, peaches, pears, plums, figs, mangoes, papayas, and nectarines—are best grilled cut in half. Firmer fruits like apples, melon slices with the rind on, oranges, lemons, limes, and grapefruit with the rinds on can be cut in half, sliced, or wedged for grilling. Clusters of grilled fruit like grapes are a wonderful addition to a cheese platter.

Even with dessert, a judicious bit of smoke flavor—from a regional wood—can add that indefinable *something*. A final drizzle of a smoked honey can do just that.

Shagbark Pineapple with Kumquat Compote
and Whipped Coconut Cream

Chocolatier's Crostini

Grilled Grape Clusters
with Brown Sugar Sour Cream

Grilled Valencia and Blood Oranges
with Honey Orange Drizzle

Grilled Papaya with Fresh Lime

Grilled Peaches with Toasted Almond Baste

Wine-Splashed Peaches, Plums, and Berries

Grilled Pound Cake
with Blueberry Cardamom Compote

Ice Cream Balls

Turtles-on-a-Stick

Somewhere over the Rainbow Ice Cream Cake

Grilled Persimmons
with Mascarpone and Spice Syrup

Grilled Brioche with Honeyed Ricotta
and Plum-Port Compote

Stars and Stripes Grilled Banana Split

Cedar-Planked Sheep's Milk Cheese
with Rummy Apricots

Prosecco Pops

Strawberry-Raspberry Pops with Lemon Balm

Peach Martini Pops

Prosecco and Ice Pop Cocktails
à la Loopy Doopy Rooftop Bar

★ ★ ★

SHAGBARK PINEAPPLE *with* KUMQUAT COMPOTE *and* WHIPPED COCONUT CREAM

When kumquats—small, oval, orange citrus fruits from Florida or California—are in season from November through March, make this easy compote to have on hand the rest of the year. It is delicious over pound cake, ice cream, or slices of pineapple (available year-round) grilled with the "bark" still on them. Put the can of coconut milk in the refrigerator at least 24 hours before you want to serve this dish so the cream easily separates from the coconut water.

Serves 4 to 6

KUMQUAT COMPOTE

1 pound (454 g) kumquat pods or the tiniest mandarin oranges you can find

2 tablespoons whole star anise (available at Asian markets or from spice companies)

2 tablespoons whole coriander seeds

1 cup (200 g) granulated sugar

1 cup (240 ml) water

SHAGBARK PINEAPPLE AND WHIPPED COCONUT CREAM

1 large ripe pineapple cut into ½-inch- (1.3 cm-) thick rounds, rind, core, and all

1 (13.4-ounce/400 ml) can full-fat coconut milk

2 tablespoons granulated sugar

2 teaspoons vanilla extract

Fresh herb sprigs, such as basil, lemon balm, or mint, for garnish

For the Kumquat Compote, cut each kumquat into fourths and remove any seeds. Place the kumquat sections, star anise, coriander, sugar, and water in a heavy saucepan over medium-high heat and bring to a boil, stirring to dissolve the sugar. Lower the heat and simmer for 15 to 20 minutes, or until the kumquat slices are glistening and translucent. Turn off the heat and let the mixture cool in the pan. Discard the whole spices, then transfer the syrup and fruit to a pint jar with a lid, making sure the fruit is covered by the syrup. Seal the jar and refrigerate. This will yield about 2 cups (474 ml), and it will keep refrigerated for several months.

For the Shagbark Pineapple, prepare a medium-hot fire in your grill. Place each pineapple round on the grill grates and grill on one side only for 2 to 3 minutes, or until it has good grill marks. Transfer to serving plates, grill-marked-side ups, and brush with a little syrup from the Kumquat Compote.

For the Whipped Coconut Cream, open the upright end of the coconut milk can and pour off the coconut water (reserve for use in soups or drinks). Scrape out the solidified coconut cream into a mixing bowl. Using an electric mixer, beat in the sugar and vanilla on low speed, then turn to high and whip until light and billowy.

To serve, place a grilled pineapple round on each plate and top with Whipped Coconut Cream in the center. Spoon some of the Kumquat Compote over all and garnish with a sprig of fresh herb.

CHOCOLATIER'S CROSTINI

This recipe is so simple yet so delicious. Grilled bread, a square of chocolate, and a sprinkle of sea salt is all you need. Use your favorite chocolate bar—perhaps from craft chocolatier Vosges in Chicago, Christopher Elbow in Kansas City and San Francisco, Mast Brothers in Brooklyn and Los Angeles, or good ol' Hershey's from Pennsylvania. We prefer dark chocolate, but if your favorite is milk chocolate, go for it. Serve with a bowl of juicy ripe strawberries or other fresh berries, if you like.

Makes 16 crostini

1 (10-inch/25 cm) baguette

6 to 8 ounces (170 to 227 g) good-quality milk, dark, or bittersweet chocolate, in bar or block form

Olive oil, for brushing

Coarse kosher salt, for sprinkling

Fresh strawberries, for serving

Prepare a medium-hot indirect fire in your grill.

Slice off the ends of the bread and then cut the bread on the diagonal into slices ½ inch (1.3 cm) thick, to get 16 slices. Break or cut the chocolate into 16 pieces. Place bread, chocolate, oil, and salt on a baking sheet and carry out to the grill.

Brush the bread with olive oil and place on the grill grates over direct heat to toast, 1 to 2 minutes. Turn the bread over and place on the indirect side of the grill. Place a piece of chocolate on each toasted side of the bread. Close the grill lid and let the bread heat for a couple of minutes, or until the chocolate begins to melt.

To serve, transfer the crostini to a platter. Sprinkle with a tiny bit of coarse salt and devour while warm, with strawberries on the side.

GRILLED GRAPE CLUSTERS
with BROWN SUGAR SOUR CREAM

So easy and yet so good! Serve the clusters on a big platter, arranged around a bowl of the sweet dipping sauce.

Serves 6 to 8

- 1 cup (240 ml) heavy whipping cream
- 1 cup (227 g) sour cream
- 2 tablespoons packed light or dark brown sugar
- 2 pounds (1 kg) seedless green and purple grape clusters

For the Brown Sugar Sour Cream, stir the cream, sour cream, and brown sugar together in a medium bowl. Let it sit at room temperature for at least 1 hour before serving.

Prepare a hot fire in your grill.

Grill the grape clusters, turning often, until you have good grill marks or scorching, about 4 to 5 minutes.

To serve, arrange the grape clusters on a platter and pass the bowl of Brown Sugar Sour Cream.

GRILLED VALENCIA *and* BLOOD ORANGES *with* HONEY ORANGE DRIZZLE

In a word, divine. This is a Florida-meets -California orange platter that is smart, healthy, and brightly flavored. The color contrast with the Valencia and blood oranges adds to the eye appeal. And if you want a final nuance of flavor, look for a smoked honey: Hickory Smoked Carolina Honey from Holy Smoke LLC in South Carolina, BBQ Blend Honey from Bay Area Bee Company, or Cherry Wood Smoked Honey from Bee Local in Oregon.

Serves 8

HONEY ORANGE DRIZZLE

2 tablespoons unsalted butter

2 tablespoons clover or smoked honey

2 teaspoons freshly grated orange zest

½ cup (120 ml) freshly squeezed orange juice

⅛ teaspoon cayenne pepper
Kosher salt

GRILLED ORANGES

4 blood oranges

4 Valencia oranges

For the Honey Orange Drizzle, melt the butter in a medium saucepan over medium-high heat. Stir in the honey and orange zest until well blended. Stir in the orange juice and remove from the heat. Stir in the cayenne pepper and salt to taste.

Prepare a hot fire in your grill.

Trim the ends off the fruit (but do not peel), and then slice into ½-inch- (1.3 cm-) thick slices. Grill the orange slices for 1 minute on each side, or until slightly browned.

To serve, arrange the orange slices, alternating Valencia and blood oranges, on a platter or individual plates and drizzle with the sauce. Serve immediately.

GRILLED PAPAYA *with* FRESH LIME

On the islands of Hawaii, Kauai, and Oahu, growing papaya on porous lava soil results in juicy, aromatic fruit. So it's only fitting that papaya gets a juicy, aromatic turn over the fire. Like most tropical fruits, papaya caramelizes easily on a hot grill, making it even more luscious.

Serves 6 to 8

¹⁄₄ cup (56 g) unsalted butter, melted

Grated zest and juice of 1 lime

¹⁄₈ teaspoon cayenne pepper

2 large ripe papayas, peeled, seeded, pitted, and cut into 2-inch (5 cm) wedges

Fresh lime wedges, for serving

Prepare a hot fire in your grill.

In a bowl, combine the melted butter, lime zest and juice, and cayenne pepper. Brush the papaya wedges with this mixture.

Grill the papaya, turning often, until you have good grill marks, about 4 to 5 minutes.

To serve, arrange on a contrasting-colored platter with fresh lime wedges.

GRILLED PEACHES
with TOASTED ALMOND BASTE

This recipe works really well with smaller northern peaches that aren't as sweet and juicy as their southern counterparts. Peaches go well with a touch of almond, and none better than the farm-to-bottle Toasted Almond Liqueur from Yahara Bay Distillery in Madison, Wisconsin. The amber liquid has an aroma of praline and marzipan, luscious with grilled peaches.

½ cup (56 g) unsalted butter

½ cup (60 ml) toasted almond liqueur or amaretto

Kosher salt

4 large firm peaches or nectarines, halved and pitted (unpeeled)

Whipped cream, for garnish

Fresh blackberries, raspberries, or blueberries, for garnish

For the Toasted Almond Baste, melt the butter in a medium saucepan over medium heat, then remove the pan from the heat and stir in the liqueur. Add just a touch of salt to bring up the flavor. Keep warm.

Prepare a medium-hot fire in your grill.

Brush the entire peach halves with baste. Place the peaches, cut-side down, on the grill and grill for 2 to 3 minutes. Baste again, then turn cut-side up, baste, and grill for 2 to 3 minutes more, or until the peaches are tender and blistered.

To serve, arrange the peach halves on a platter or portion onto individual dessert plates. Dollop the peaches with whipped cream in the middle and scatter with berries.

WINE-SPLASHED PEACHES, PLUMS, and BERRIES

Sometimes, after a heavier barbecue meal, you want dessert to be very light—and grill-flavor-free. This delectable concoction, featuring farm-fresh fruits and berries, delivers. The combination of the wine and an almond-flavored liqueur is marvelous, and the citrus juice keeps the fruit from oxidizing.

Makes 6 to 8 servings

4 ripe peaches, peeled, pitted, and diced

4 ripe plums, peeled, pitted, and diced

1 cup (240 ml) sweet white or red wine, such as an Alsatian riesling

¼ cup (60 ml) amaretto or other almond-flavored liqueur

2 tablespoons granulated sugar

2 teaspoons freshly squeezed lemon or lime juice

6 ounces (170 g) fresh raspberries

3 tablespoons sliced almonds

Fresh mint sprigs, for garnish

Place the peaches and plums in a large glass bowl.

In a separate bowl, combine the wine, amaretto, sugar, and lemon juice; mix well. Pour the wine mixture over the peaches and plums and stir. Cover and chill for 1 hour.

Just before serving, add the raspberries and almonds, gently folding them into the mixture so that the raspberries stay whole and intact.

To serve, gently ladle the fruit into individual glass bowls and garnish with a sprig of mint.

GRILLED POUND CAKE
with BLUEBERRY CARDAMOM COMPOTE

You'll be amazed how wonderful grilled pound cake tastes. Topped with aromatic blueberry compote, all it needs is a scoop of your favorite ice cream or frozen yogurt.

Serves 6

BLUEBERRY CARDAMOM COMPOTE

¹/₄ cup (60 ml) water

12 ounces (340 g) fresh blueberries

¹/₃ cup (67 g) granulated sugar

¹/₂ teaspoon ground cardamom

Juice of half a lemon

GRILLED POUND CAKE

1 loaf store-bought pound cake, cut into 6 thick slices

Ice cream or frozen yogurt, for serving

Fresh mint sprigs, for garnish

For the Blueberry Cardamom Compote, place the water, blueberries, sugar, and cardamom in a medium saucepan over medium heat and bring to a boil. Reduce the heat, stirring occasionally, and simmer for 10 minutes, or until the blueberries have plumped up and turned a shiny dark blue. Remove from the heat and stir in the lemon juice. Set aside.

Prepare a medium-hot fire in your grill.

Grill the pound cake slices for 1 minute on each side, or until each slice has good grill marks.

To serve, arrange a slice of grilled pound cake on each dessert plate. Spoon the Blueberry Cardamom Compote over the slice of grilled cake, add a scoop of ice cream, and garnish with a fresh mint sprig.

·——— Ice Cream Balls and Cakes ———·

After a summer cookout, ice cream desserts are a welcome way to cool off and take a break from the heat—and the flavor—of the grill. Home-churned ice cream is always a favorite, especially if there is a designated ice and salt person in charge of churning. Easier alternatives to the churned ice cream are these delicious cold treats made with premium store-bought ice cream. They can be fancy and colorful with sprinkles and mini-chocolate chips, covered with cookie crumbs, or served with chocolate, caramel, or fruit sauce. Make, plate, sauce, and serve!

ICE CREAM BALLS

Our friend and restaurateur Jasper Mirabile serves tartufo (ice cream balls) at Jasper's, his family's Italian restaurant in Kansas City. The size of a tennis ball, these frozen ice cream treats, rolled in chocolate cookie crumbs, are plated on top of chocolate sauce and served with a big fat frozen strawberry on the side.

Serves 8

24 Oreo-style chocolate
   sandwich cookies, crumbled
   in a food processor
8 large scoops of vanilla bean
   ice cream, from about ¹/₂
   gallon (1.8 kg)
8 large strawberries, frozen,
   for garnish

WARM CHOCOLATE SAUCE

¹/₂ cup (120 ml) heavy
   whipping cream
²/₃ cup (115 g) semisweet
   chocolate chips

Spread the cookie crumbs in a large casserole dish. Roll the ice cream scoops in the crumbs until well coated. Place an inch (2.5 cm) apart on a dish and set in the freezer for at least 8 hours ahead of serving or 1 to 2 days ahead.

For the Warm Chocolate Sauce, pour the cream into a large glass measuring cup and microwave for about 1¹/₂ minutes, or until just beginning to boil. (Watch the cream so you can stop the microwave before it boils over.) Add the chocolate chips and let sit for 5 minutes. Slowly stir until the sauce is dark and creamy.

When ready to serve, spoon a portion of the chocolate sauce on a plate and top with an ice cream ball. Garnish with a frozen strawberry.

TURTLES-ON-A-STICK

Turtle chocolates, with their creamy caramel filling and pecans, originated in Chicago. The best take on these chocolates is in an ice cream flavor from Baskin-Robbins. Purchase their Caramel Turtle Truffle Ice Cream. It's vanilla ice cream laced with caramel and miniature chocolate turtles, and it's a mouthful of perfection. This recipe is for our dear friend Al Saroni, Jr., who introduced us to this flavor.

Serves 10

24 Oreo-style chocolate sandwich cookies

¹/₂ cup (65 g) pecans

10 scoops Caramel Turtle Truffle ice cream, about ¹/₂ gallon (1.8 kg)

10 wooden ice cream sticks

Smoked honey, for serving (optional)

Place the cookies and pecans in a food processor and pulse until they are fine crumbs.

Spread the crumb mixture in a large casserole dish. Roll the ice cream scoops in the crumbs until well coated. Return the crumbed ice cream balls to the casserole dish, placed 1 inch (2.5 cm) apart. Insert an ice cream stick into the center of each ball. Freeze for at least 8 hours before serving. If you like, serve each Turtle-on-a-Stick in a small pool of smoked honey on individual dessert plates.

SOMEWHERE OVER THE RAINBOW ICE CREAM CAKE

Karen's niece, Jenny Peterson, is an ice cream cake-oholic, and for good reason. Ice cream cakes are easy to make and can feature your favorite flavor and color combinations, but you do need to allow several hours for them to firm up before serving. Even better, make the cake a day or two ahead, wrap, and freeze. The cake keeps for a month in the freezer, covered well. If you like, serve it with a spoonful of Warm Chocolate Sauce (page 182), Kumquat Compote (page 170), Blueberry Cardamom Compote (page 181), or Fresh Raspberry Sauce (from Ruby Slipper Beets, page 144) drizzled over the top.

Serves 8 to 10

- 1 quart (567 g) strawberry, raspberry, or boysenberry ice cream
- 1 quart (567 g) golden vanilla or buttered pecan ice cream
- 1 quart (567 g) pistachio or mint chocolate chip ice cream
- 36 vanilla sandwich cookies, or 48 vanilla wafers
- ¼ cup (56 g) unsalted butter, melted

Preheat the oven to 350°F (177°C).

Set the ice cream containers on the kitchen counter for 15 to 20 minutes to soften.

Place the cookies in a food processor and pulse until crumbly. With the motor running, add the melted butter until blended. Press the cookie mixture into a 9-inch (23 cm) springform pan. Bake for 10 minutes and let cool.

Spoon each ice cream into the pan and smooth the top before adding the next. Freeze for at least 6 hours. Cut into slices and serve.

GRILLED PERSIMMONS *with* MASCARPONE *and* SPICE SYRUP

In the fall, native persimmons turn orange when they ripen but are full of seeds and too soft to grill. Asian Fuyu persimmons, first brought from Japan to California by Commodore Perry in 1856, stay firm and don't have a core or seeds. They can be cut in half and lightly grilled to bring out their natural sweetness. Serve them with a dollop of mascarpone and aromatic Spice Syrup.

Serves 6

SPICE SYRUP

2 tablespoons mixed whole spices, such as allspice, cloves, star anise, coriander seeds, and Szechuan peppercorns

$^{1}/_{2}$ cup (120 ml) boiling water

$^{3}/_{4}$ cup (150 g) granulated sugar

GRILLED PERSIMMONS WITH MASCARPONE

6 ripe Fuyu persimmons, halved

1 (8-ounce/227 g) container mascarpone

Fresh thyme sprigs, for garnish

For the Spice Syrup, scatter the whole spices in a small skillet over medium heat and toast, gently shaking the pan, until you can just start to smell their aroma, about 2 minutes. Do not let them smoke. Pour the boiling water into a small bowl and add the toasted spices. Cover and let infuse for at least 2 hours at room temperature.

Strain the spice water into a microwave-safe bowl and stir in the sugar. (Let the whole spices dry on a paper towel, then cover and store them for two to three more uses.) Microwave on high for 2 minutes, or until the sugar has dissolved and the syrup is aromatic. Use right away or store in a small jar in the refrigerator for up to 3 months.

Prepare a medium-hot fire in your grill.

Grill the persimmons, cut-side down, for 2 to 3 minutes, or until they have good grill marks.

To serve, place two persimmon halves on each plate, dollop with mascarpone, and drizzle with Spice Syrup. Garnish with fresh sprigs of thyme.

GRILLED BRIOCHE *with* HONEYED RICOTTA *and* PLUM-PORT COMPOTE

Brioche is a very rich, buttery bread, making it a perfect dessert choice. It will grill quickly, so make sure you attend to it and don't let it burn. The Plum-Port Compote makes plenty, and if you have any left over, use it for breakfast the next morning.

Serves 6 to 8

PLUM-PORT COMPOTE

1 pound (454 g) purple
   plums, pitted and sliced

1/2 cup (120 ml) port

2 tablespoons granulated sugar

**GRILLED BRIOCHE
WITH HONEYED
RICOTTA**

1 (12-ounce/340 g) container
   ricotta

1/4 cup (60 ml) clover honey

12 slices brioche

Fresh orange mint or lemon
   balm sprigs, for garnish

For the Plum-Port Compote, place the plums, port, and sugar in a medium saucepan over medium-high heat. Bring to a boil, then reduce the heat and simmer, stirring occasionally, for 10 minutes, or until the plums are soft, glistening, and purple all the way through. Remove from the heat and set aside.

Prepare a medium-hot fire in your grill.

Combine the ricotta and honey in a small bowl and set aside.

Grill the brioche on one side only for about 1 minute, or until it has good grill marks.

To serve, spread the grilled surface with the honeyed ricotta and set on a plate. Spoon the Plum-Port Compote over the top and garnish with herb sprigs.

STARS *and* STRIPES
GRILLED BANANA SPLIT

Back when drug-store soda fountains were the movers and shakers in casual food, an apprentice pharmacist invented the banana split in 1904. This distinctly American, more-is-more concoction featured a banana, split down the middle, with three kinds of ice cream and three different ice cream sauces, plus nuts and whipped cream. Today, grilling bananas takes the classic banana split to a deliciously new level, and the backyard version of this dish relies more on fresh and less on excess. Buy bright yellow, still-firm bananas to grill. Try our homemade Warm Chocolate Sauce (page 182) instead of store-bought hot fudge.

Serves 4

4 bananas

1 quart (1 kg) good-quality vanilla ice cream or frozen yogurt

6 ounces (170 g) fresh blueberries

6 ounces (170 g) fresh raspberries

1 (18-ounce/510 g) jar good-quality hot fudge sauce, warmed, or 1 recipe Warm Chocolate Sauce (page 182)

Prepare a medium-hot fire in your grill.

Slice the bananas in half lengthwise, leaving the skin on.

Place the bananas, cut-side down, on the grill grates and grill for 2 to 3 minutes, or until the bananas have good grill marks.

To serve, remove the banana skins and place two banana halves, grilled-side up, in each of four banana split dishes or ice cream bowls. Set two scoops of ice cream on top of each serving. Scatter with blueberries and raspberries and drizzle with hot fudge sauce.

CEDAR-PLANKED SHEEP'S MILK CHEESE *with* RUMMY APRICOTS

As the nights get cooler, bundle up and sit outside under the stars, around the fire pit or the outdoor fireplace, and enjoy the company of friends and family. As a last sweet bite, stir up a batch of Rummy Apricots and then slather them over fresh sheep's milk cheese that tastes both opulent and tangy, a fine canvas for equally opulent and tangy apricots, aromatic cedar, and heady rum. Try a Brebis Blanche from 3-Corner Field in New York, Fresh Nettle from Green Dirt Farm in Missouri, or Honey and Lavender Driftless from Hidden Springs Creamery in Wisconsin. This dish will take on a burnished appearance and have the aromatic flavor of the wood plank. If you like, enhance the look of falling leaves with a scattering of pistachios and fresh sage leaves once off the grill. Serve the cheese right on the plank and pass a basket of baguette slices and crisp apple wedges.

Serves 8

RUMMY APRICOTS

¼ cup (60 ml) dark rum

2 ounces (57 g) dried apricots, snipped into small pieces

1 cup (227 g) apricot preserves

CEDAR-PLANKED SHEEP'S MILK CHEESE

2 (8-ounce/227 g) rounds soft sheep's milk cheese

½ cup (65 g) roasted, shelled pistachios

8 fresh sage leaves

Baguette slices, for serving

2 apples, cored and cut into wedges, for serving

For the Rummy Apricots, combine the rum and dried apricots in a small bowl and let them sit for 30 minutes to hydrate the dried fruit. In a saucepan, combine the rum, dried apricots, and apricot preserves. Cook over medium heat, stirring, until the ingredients combine, about 5 minutes. Remove from the heat.

Prepare a hot indirect fire in your grill.

Place the 2 rounds of cheese on the plank and slather with the Rummy Apricots.

Place the plank on the indirect side of the grill and close the lid. Plank for 20 to 25 minutes, or until the Brie is just starting to soften and the apricot topping has a burnished appearance.

Serve on the plank sprinkled with the pistachios and sage leaves. Pass a basket of baguette slices and crisp apple wedges.

Popsicles

Does everyone know the story about how popsicles were first made?
Here is a nod to Frank Epperson of Oakland, California, who accidentally left a glass of powdered soda and water with a stick in it outside on a cold night in 1905. It was first called an epsicle and later called "frozen ice on a stick" when it was patented in 1923. Another version of the story is that it became "popsicle" when his children referred to it as Pop's "sicle." Whatever you call it, it is good, especially on a hot day when you're cooking dinner on a hot grill.

Our recipes include some with alcohol and some that you serve in a glass of prosecco—very grown-up! On a trip to New York City, we celebrated Judith's birthday with ice pop cocktails at Loopy Doopy Rooftop Bar in the Conrad Hotel in Lower Manhattan.

You need to purchase a standard set of bar-shaped molds that come with sticks. You can purchase additional sticks, too. Like most things, they are best if not left too long in the freezer, so freeze for only 1 week tops. To unmold the pops, run hot water over the outsides of the molds for a few seconds, then gently pull the pops out by holding onto the sticks.

PROSECCO POPS

When making pops, it's always faster if your ingredients are cold. Pour a cup of prosecco into a bowl the day before you make these so that it's flat when you use it. Set the bowl in the refrigerator.

Serves 6

- 1 cup (240 ml) cranberry-grape juice
- 1 cup (240 ml) flat prosecco
- 1 cup (80 ml) water
- 1 teaspoon freshly grated lemon zest
- 1½ tablespoons freshly squeezed lemon juice

Combine all the ingredients in a pitcher or bowl, fill the ice pop molds, and insert the sticks. Freeze for at least 8 hours.

STRAWBERRY-RASPBERRY POPS
with LEMON BALM

If you don't have lemon balm, substitute fresh mint.

Serves 6

2 cups (340 g) fresh raspberries

3 cups (340 g) chopped fresh strawberries

1/3 cup (80 ml) water

2 tablespoons freshly squeezed lime juice

1 teaspoon freshly grated lime zest

2 tablespoons finely chopped fresh lemon balm

In a blender, purée the berries, water, and lime juice.

Using a wooden spoon, push the mixture through a strainer into a pitcher or large bowl and discard the solids. Add the lime zest and lemon balm. Pour into the ice pop molds and insert the sticks. Freeze for at least 8 hours.

PEACH MARTINI POPS

Bellini meets frozen martini in this adults-only take on the classic Popsicle. Just the thing to enjoy while you're babysitting that brisket or pork butt outside on a hot day.

Serves 6

1 1/2 pounds (680 g) very ripe peaches

1/3 cup (67 g) granulated sugar

2 tablespoons vodka

2 teaspoons freshly grated lemon zest

1 1/2 tablespoons freshly squeezed lemon juice

Peel the peaches, pit them, and cut them into chunks.

Place the peaches, sugar, vodka, lemon zest, and lemon juice in a blender and purée. Pour into the ice pop molds and insert the sticks. Freeze for at least 8 hours.

PROSECCO AND ICE POP COCKTAILS
à la LOOPY DOOPY ROOFTOP BAR

You need a wide-mouth stemmed glass or a tall double old-fashioned for this cocktail so that it holds the prosecco and when the ice pop is inserted, the liquid doesn't pour over the glass. In a hurry and don't have time to make your own pops? We recommend paletas, Mexican popsicles made with real fruit and juices. You can find paletas in many unusual flavors—blackberry, guava, coconut, and more—at Hispanic grocery stores or paleterias.

Serves 1

Chilled prosecco

1 wide-mouth red wine glass, or a tall double old-fashioned, chilled

1 ice pop, homemade or store-bought

Pour the prosecco into the chilled glass about half full. Set an ice pop into the prosecco. Cheers!

Index